T0121850

ISLAM
THE ALIEN FAITH

Hadi F. Eid

Order this book online at www.trafford.com
or email orders@trafford.com

Most Trafford titles are also available at major online book retailers.

© Copyright 2013 Hadi F. Eid.
All rights reserved. No part of this publication may be reproduced, stored in a retrieval
system, or transmitted, in any form or by any means, electronic, mechanical, photocopying,
recording, or otherwise, without the written prior permission of the author.

Printed in the United States of America.

ISBN: 978-1-4669-7908-6 (sc)
ISBN: 978-1-4669-7907-9 (e)

Library of Congress Control Number: 2013904282

Trafford rev. 03/06/2013

 www.trafford.com

North America & international
toll-free: 1 888 232 4444 (USA & Canada)
phone: 250 383 6864 ♦ fax: 812 355 4082

Contents

"Islam started alien and will return as alien as it started, blessed are the aliens."

Muhammad

ONE

Foreword

What does exactly mean to be a Muslim today? And is Islam much more a religion than an inherited and cherished state of mind? At the dawn of the third millennium the Muslim personality is searching for its identity while bracing to take the globalization superhighway.

The West may be fond of its technical achievements, the Far East may brag about its economical miracles, but Muslims are preoccupied more than anything in arguing who they really are and what their heritage has been. Throughout that quarrelling, dueling essays fill the airs and the papers in defense of Islam and rarely stray far from the initial frontlines that had energized it from the start.

One may devote a lifetime peeling back the onion skins as so many scholars have done to unravel the real Islam and tell it apart from the traditionally inherited faith. Throughout this long travail and no matter where Muslims stop they encounter the same basic question that framed their history: what is the Real Islam.

Revisionists may eventually retrace the true history. Their engagement in ceaseless pursuit of midcourse correction to get Islam into its modern track without becoming a tyranny in the process is nowadays their prime concentration. Slowly but surely rationalization is digging its transparent path through the many somber veils of postulates. The Muslim mind, hard hit by its contagious environment of facts and figures is being ushered into the domain of logic and pushed with a waste-not approach to the realm of reason.

Diverse interpretations of the Islamic history will inevitably be proposed in the coming decades while traditional cultural distinctions around the world continue to dissolve. As the population of the Muslim world keeps on growing and with it an educated feminism revival the early historical sources shall continue to be scrutinized. With the diversity of interpretations will surely come increased fractiousness, perhaps intensified by the fact that Islam now exists in such a great variety of social and intellectual settings: Bosnia, Iran, Indonesia, Nigeria, Saudi Arabia, South Africa, the United States and so on. More than ever before, anybody wishing to understand global affairs will need to understand Islamic civilization in all its permutations. Surely the best way to start is with the study of the Koran which promises in the years ahead to be more contentious, fascinating and significant.

Differences between ongoing academic theories and daily practices of Islam around the world are huge. The majority of Muslims are unlikely to query the orthodox understanding of the Koran and Islamic history. Yet Islam became one of the world's great religions in part not because of its openness but rather its acceptance to social changes and new ideas. Further openness would be at hand only when it relinquishes its fundamental orthodoxy and gives the mind its free reigns of thinking. It happened in Baghdad under Caliph Haroon Alrashid and in Andalusia with philosopher Ibn Rushd. It fits to remember that when Europe was mired in feudal Dark Ages the sages of a flourishing Islamic civilization opened an era of great scientific and philosophical sighting. The ideas of the ancient Greeks and Romans might never have been introduced to Europe were it not for the Islamic historians and philosophers who rediscovered and revived them. Islam's own history shows that the prevailing conception of the Koran is not the only one ever to have existed and the recent history of biblical scholarship shows that not all their studies are antagonistic. They can instead be carried out with the aim of spiritual and cultural regeneration.

For more than a century there have been public figures in the Islamic world who have attempted the revisionist study of the Islamic history. Unfortunately enough these were the first casualties of this endeavor: the exiled Egyptian professor Nasr Abu Zaid is not unique. His most famous predecessor was the prominent Egyptian education minister, university professor and author Taha Hussein, the 'Pillar of Arabic Literature' who devoted himself to study the pre-Islamic Arabian poetry. He ended up concluding that much of that body of work had been fabricated well after the establishment of Islam in order to lend outside support to Koranic mythology.

Abu Zaid also cites the enormously influential Muhammad Abdu as a precursor. A nineteenth-century father of Egyptian modernism, Abdu saw the potential for a new Islamic theology in the theories of the ninth-century Mu'tazilis whose ideas gained popularity in some Muslim circles early in the last century leading another Egyptian intellectual, Ahmad Amin to remark in 1936 that "the demise of Mu'tazilism was the greatest misfortune to have afflicted Muslims as with them the development of a complex theology based partly on a metaphorical rather than simply literal understanding of the Koran was aborted."

Unfortunately Taha Hussein, like Nasr Abu Zaid was declared an apostate in Egypt; Abu Zaid advocated reinterpretation of the Koran for the modern age, "so that once more it becomes productive for the essence of our culture and arts which are being strangled in our society." His book, *The Concept of the Text* (1990), largely responsible for his exile from Egypt has gone through at least eight underground printings in Cairo and Beirut.

Another scholar, Muhammad Arkoun the Algerian professor at the University of Paris, argued in *Lectures du Coran* (1982), that "it is time Islam assumes, along with all of the great cultural traditions, the modern risks of scientific knowledge," and suggested that "the problem of the divine authenticity of the Koran can serve to reactivate Islamic thought and engage it in the major debates of our age."

He regrets that most Muslims are unaware that different conceptions of the Koran exist within their own historical tradition. Re-examination offers an opportunity to challenge the orthodoxy from within rather than having to rely on "hostile" outside sources. Arkoun, Abu Zaid, and others hoped that this exercise will ultimately lead to nothing less than an Islamic renaissance.

The time for Islamic introspection tackling this 'challenge from within' has come. Muslim clerics should remember that Christianity across the ages had run through a good deal of 'God copy editing' to dispel orthodox applications of the scriptures. A little more than a century ago the biblical scholar John William Burgon said: "The Bible is none other than *the voice of Him that sits upon the Throne!* Every Book of it, every Chapter of it, every Verse of it, every Word of it, every Syllable of it . . . every Letter of it, is the direct utterance of the Most High!"

Not all Christian clerics think this way about the Bible. The orthodox Muslim view of the Koran as self-evidently the Word of God, perfect and inimitable in message, language, style, and form, is strikingly similar to the fundamentalist Christian notion of the Bible's "inerrancy" and "verbal inspiration" that is not common in many places today. The closest analogue of Christian belief to the role of the Koran in Muslim belief is not the Bible but "Christ, the Word of God made flesh and the Koran, the Word of God made text." Questioning its sanctity or authority is thus considered an outright attack on Islam.

The mainly secular effort to reinterpret the Koran based in part on textual evidence distinguishing between basic, circumstantial and added fragments is disturbing and offensive to many Muslims; just as attempts to reinterpret the Bible and the life of Jesus are disturbing and offensive to many conservative Christians. There are scholars, Muslims among them, who feel that such an effort which amounts essentially to placing the Koran in history will provide fuel for an Islamic revival of sorts; a re-appropriation of tradition and a going forward by looking back. Thus far confined to scholarly argument, this sort of thinking can be very powerful and as the histories of the Renaissance and the Reformation demonstrate, can lead to major social changes. The Koran after all is currently the world's most ideologically influential text.

This 'challenge from within' is a must and is bound to happen; it would help put the Western assault on Islam at bay. It is the assault of the powerful on the powerless and the frustration of the "rational" towards the "superstitious". The West coordinated the powers of the State, integrated Academia, harnessed the Church and looked with dismay at the defective citadel of Islam. There he threw streaks of arrogance, rationalism and domineering fantasy. The East was only the avid recipient and consumer of this merchandise and Muslims found themselves absorbed day and night in Western ways of life—and thinking. The gap widened dangerously between the *actor* who won all opportunities and the *reactor* who lost all initiatives. A seemingly unholy conspiracy to dislodge the Muslim's sacred heritage and address a dare-devil venture to the utmost trophy: the Muslim mind itself.

Reason and rationale should be adopted rid this mind of such assaults. Islam then would cease to be the Muslims' dilemma to become their salute. A Muslim should not be confounded in the historical authenticity of his faith that can happen only when he drops many old postulates and inferred fragments of his scripture that belongs to a different past. Muslim consciousness must be made to accept the cognitive certainty of the basic revealed message. A revised, time-honored and conciliatory reconsideration of the Koranic structure would reinforce its universal mission, appease the challenge of the global domination and retrace its respected position among world communities.

The book you are about to read is an on-the-fence, historical and factual penetration to Islam as supported by many historic and Koranic facts. The writer's main interest is to rid the besieged Muslim mind from the many outdated postulates and unleash it to openness and sincerity. Readers will encounter poignant facts, revealing narrations and candid stories. Earth will not shudder and Heaven will not fall at the many encounters with the truth but a fresh knowledge will ensue and cause the fall of many tyrannical codes, exactly as the Kaaba idols had fallen earlier under the axe of Muhammad.

TWO

A Mind under Siege

"Every free nation should train its children to think, encourage them to research and release their freedom to unleash their personal opinions. A fanatic teacher imposing his own theories grooms restricted minds. Any nation adopting this educational system produces stagnant individuals unable to soar and progress."

Sydney Haskin—Manchester University

It is amazing what ancient wilderness could produce: God's miracles as well as His strikes were performed there. The angels came down over saints in the darkness of the night and hermits could only contemplate in their remote caverns. The ghostly loneliness of the desert is inconceivable: It poses no obstacles to belief. The Bedouin shudders by any shadow of doubt in the Almighty, overall Master of the Universe. In the desert sight spreads out unrestrained to the infinite, the boundless . . . to deity. Vastness of the desert unfolds under the feet and overhead indefinitely; all there is between heavens and earth is limitless.

The Bedouin of yesteryears was restless and agoraphobic; his surrounding did not allow him to stabilize himself and improve his entity. He was keen about his tightly wrapped legacy and this is where he liked to live. Any evolution around him was related to universal laws not to his own endeavors. The deeper he plunged in the past with his family tree the more secure he would feel; otherwise he was a rootless branch blown by the desert wind . . .

His attachment to the past was his shield against all hazards. He was eternally subjected to fear: he dreaded the rain and the drought; stay put or go nomad. He feared the sands under his tent or the stars above his head. He hated storms as well as tranquility and was alarmed by foreigners as much as his own kin. This diversified fear enforced the pillars of his belief and made him reluctant to change let alone revise his religious principles. He maintained that his religion rolled down from Abraham, Moses and Jesus. His belief was the one of "the People of the Book" without segregation. His God is the one of "Beni Israel" before they subdivided into various factions. His book is an incorporation of all ancient Holy Books. Thus, Islam is the religion of unison par excellence with equal integration among all preceding prophets; a preconceived formula to restore peace of mind and fearless worshipping.

This fear is inherited and experienced by all Muslims today. It remains the single, most intense factor in a Muslim life. He who does not fear may not be counted among good Muslims. This crucial fear is centered mostly on God's deity. Hence the repetitive plea: "Allah o Akbar"—God is greater—for fear that God may not be so. God's 99 glorifying names are always pronounced with related attributes: "the exalted", "the venerated", "the elevated" . . . The fear of God necessitates His highness, might and remoteness; His throne atop the seventh heaven or over the sea waves. Any casual or indifferent mentioning of His name would crack the foundations of the universe . . .

This fear when examined, serves to shield the Muslim away from doubt. Only the free and fearless scrutinizes and deduces while the fearful incarcerates behind all locks and bolts to reach self appeasement: he attaches his faith to the pillars of heavens; binds it to the angels. His covenant with God for all mundane predicaments renders all other researches and solutions obsolete. Shrinking the narrow grounds to deduction yields wider grounds to tranquility.

The eternal quest for contentment requires complete adherence to the revealed Book; personal lifestyles, social ways and means are at their best when ascribed by the Book. Every new philosophy or theory is meaningless if not supported by the Scripture and doomed to repudiation. This tranquility spared its followers efforts to devise and create: they know the Book in all verses, all God's names, and the expected delights of Paradise; their knowledge bestowed peace on them: every problem has a solution and every question an answer.

Within this restful and serene realm everything is stable except the man; he is the living victim of such serenity. It looks as if Allah assigned his Prophet, revealed his scripture . . . and vanished; no inquiry or reconsideration; only irrevocable postulates.

The plight of the Muslim mind lies here: what a modern Muslim *thinks* as opposed to what he is being *dictated*. Perhaps the most tormenting impasse for a man is to possess an astute mind that he cannot put to optimum use. The Muslim discerning mind is appalled by the dreadful behavior of other fellow Muslims. He terms it wrong but remains restrained to voice a contradicting opinion.

Many books have been written on and about Islam; very few against it. There were even fewer in-depth analyses answerable to today's mind. Modern Muslims are at a loss to comprehend the unfathomed causes of their problems, struggles and disparities. They do know however most of their deficiencies are related to concepts and inspirations of Islam's early eras still going on unabashed.

As we said earlier, many modern Islamic scholars are trying hard to untangle their faith from such antiquated dogmas. Their attempt to inject into Islam what Europe did earlier to Christianity is not working. The many hurdles ahead do not seem surmountable. Islam is not just a spiritual faith but a doctrine for the day-to-day mundane life. Religious scribes or Ulemas have a tremendous dilemma: keep the scripture intact and with it their own standing or revise it and be deemed unfaithful. Followers suffer the same plight: they either have to adhere to Ulemas' fatwas (resolutions) enforcing ongoing conservatism, or risk alienation.

The model Muslim country that achieved separation between old faith and contemporary life is Turkey. Yet this uncertain separation is challenged frequently through mosques' pulpits and streets demonstrations. Turkey endures an eternal inner and outer struggle of two creeds: Muhammad's and Ataturk's. One watched by the Koranic verses, the other by the armed forces. How and for how long this will drag or which will prevail is anybody's guess. This country whose religion is Islam is not a dictatorship but a democracy still far from perfect at a transitory time where women are allowed again to wear the head scarf. A modern European paradigm of Islam and in many ways the heir of the Romans is shifting gradually to Islamic dictates. To enable Arabic-illiterate Turkish women perform their prayers the Mufti of Turkey Raheeb Aglou released recently a fatwa allowing them to recite the Koran in Turkish; which encouraged the Berber Mufti of Morocco to a similar step in Berber language. These unprecedented moves triggered the rage of Ulemas in Cairo Azhar University the most trusted religious authority in the Muslim world, who branded such a move as 'Budaa' (heretic novelty) defined summarily in Islam: "a 'Budaa' is an aberration; any aberration is doomed to hellfire".

Other 'modern' Muslim nations are not as lucky in creative achievements. They go on commingling religion and politics to the point that the governance lines are blurred. Their modernization schemes are led by hesitant and dispersed individuals hardly supported by state-owned media where Islam is the official 'state religion'. They are encouraged by many in secrecy but largely ignored and loathed in the open. Those daring souls among them who spoke out revisionism were either exiled or declared apostates.

Clearly the Muslim mind is mystified. Torn between the traditional reflections of Bedouin concepts produced in the life and times of Muhammad and his followers and the modern dictates of the 21st. century. Muslims may modernize their lifestyles only at the cost of setting aside enormous parts of the Koran, Hadith and Sinna (Prophet's talks and teachings). These three elements constitute together the inseparable structure of the faith. They are untouchable and heretofore away from any renovation: "do not add (to the doctrine) nor append," said Muhammad, "you have been fulfilled."

Throughout Islam's religious history in the Middle East Muslims were victims to a heightened and endless mayhem. Clerics established a set of assumptions they derived from God's disclosures as well as those of the Prophet, his followers and subsequent Caliphs (Muhammad's legatees). They attributed to God all miseries and fortitudes and reinterpreted in His name all books and revelations. In His name they killed their fellow men overtly to defend His name and furtively to safeguard and boost their dogmatic subdivisions. Those convictions were not confined to the Middle East area but exported to many places around the globe.

To the Muslim mind it is a limited and unfortunate parameter where all thoughts, opinions and judgments should roll around not only religious matters but worldly issues as well. Therefore a devout Muslim, let alone an extremist, may not carry out an unconventional discussion or voice a liberated opinion no matter how the topics are unrelated to faith. His mind is always bound to the inflexible inner ordains carefully programmed and regularly updated in his subconscious mind.

The dilemma is tremendous: the Koran and Sinna may only be strictly followed—or dropped altogether. No amendments have been attempted to this day. The Arabic language is the richest living tongue in metaphors. Allah's ninety nine names are all allegoric. To this date one can use poetic metaphors on any given subject to formulate a statement that can be construed in various ways. Muhammad, allegedly called the "illiterate Prophet", was an accomplished language authority. "Eloquence brings magic" he used to boast. His sermons remain today masterpieces of persuasiveness. The rhymed and rhythmic Koran language delivered Allah's message across a poetic bridge of eloquence. Its verses (or "Ayahs": godly signs), are not meant to be read but piously crooned and vocalized. As any poetic verses rarely a word can be called off or substituted. Here lies a colossal obstacle for any attempt to update the faith.

Deeply aware of this enclosure, Islamic scribes as well as scholars propagate that their faith encompasses all basic life elements of culture, knowledge, legal system, doctrine and other guidelines. M. Shamsuddine, a leading Muslim cleric insists and is echoed by many scholars that Islam "contains a complete order for life that does not prerequisite any other order; the Islamic Sharia (bylaws) covers and contains all legal standards for the living of man". He adds: "Koran legislation comes from God Almighty; it is the perfect order to establish pure societies enabling men to pursue their progressive goals".

He concludes that: "man should be *forbidden* to seek any other betterment or remodeling: Islam is the mould that turns out the shape of the world."

Much ahead of him, Shahrazori, the most trusted Imam in Hadith said: "Philosophy is the base for all insolence, corrosion and mischief. Whoever resorts to it deviates from the right path of Sharia . . . as to logic; it is the access to philosophy. Access to evil is also evil. It is therefore the duty of any Muslim ruler to catch any of those who choose the routes of philosophical researches and take them to Islam or the sword." (Dr. A. Badawi—Kuwait Printing Agency).

Shahrazori is probably excusable in saying what he said 800 years ago. The Bedouin is an innate foe to philosophy, logic and whatever broadens and educates the mind; and a natural friend to emotions, poetry, war, hunting, glorifying, befriending, revenging and all those attributes that conciliate and soothe his mind. Until this day philosophy and logic are banned from curriculums in many schools across the Muslim world including philosophers like the Andalusian Ibn Rushd; he produced good material to liberate the Muslim mind at a fleeting civilized time away from fundamentalism. Ibn Rushd was later exiled and his books burnt.

Modern Muslims suffer a constrained state in this pond of thinking: all successes or failures, deprivation or abundance, health or sickness, virility or impotence, even promptness or tardiness . . . are related to Allah. "Inshalla" or "God willing" is the favorite, irrevocable justification for all would-be failures: It is uttered when given a military order, promising a deadline or preparing a cup of tea! The Christian "Faith in God" is opposed to Islam's "Complete Reliance on God."

Jesus elevated men to be "the sons of God;" Islam maintained the pre-Islamic, idolatry designation as "His slaves" in an absolute dependence on the Almighty.

Allah and His prophet form a unified source of faith. The Islamic scripture insisted on this duet and repeatedly mentioned it in the Koran to bestow on Muhammad the infallible status. Thus the prophet is a "closer sovereign over all believers than their own souls", the overall custodian of their destiny, wealth, women and children; one who shares with God the supreme judging authority on all mankind in this world and the hereafter.

Today's Muslim is distraught to see the world around him moving from one achievement to another while he watches, captive of his own antiquated shell. He is sick of the long list of old fashioned Halal-permissible—and Haram-forbidden—guidelines governing his daily life according to erstwhile rules on how to greet or talk or wash or handle sex. He is dismayed in the absence of Muslims' achievements and inventions where they are unable to manufacture a computer chip or a car spare part. True, he is proud of his ancestors and recognized thinkers such as Ibn Al-Haytham and Ibn Sina who practiced primitive medicine and Ibn Hayan who formulated algebra as well as Al-Khawarezmi who raised the power of a base number to produce a given number, a process the West barrowed in his name, "logarithm" and developed to produce today's computing.

But where is the modern contribution of Islam today? What kind of life would the Muslim countries have if westerners had not discovered oil in their lands and used their technology to exploit it? He is angry to see himself immersed in the western civilization while he enjoys the comforts produced by western minds. He sees the sharp contrast between the social and economic conditions in Europe, America and the Far East where societies were founded on the basis of liberated minds and those conditions in many Islamic countries. He is angrier to see his clerics curse western civilization and portray it as the new crusade invading their prestigious heritage.

He is cheerless to see himself among millions of Muslims frayed between the pursuit of happiness and the glum pullback to old schemes. He is in an apprehensive, merciless hunt for the Truth and God; while they shimmer like a mirage in his eyes he watches his ever relaxed clerics nonchalantly living with both. He comprehends and values the teachings of the Prophet and his retinue yet he contends—only with his own self—these were normal men whose endeavors could have been right or wrong. As such, why their teachings should wrap up today's problems and affairs, science and literature, schools and institutions, present and future? These were men who lived, suffered, enjoyed, spoke wisdom, uttered foolishness and passed away. Their legacy may remain alive but only as broad directives not tapered principles. They were devout and committed but one could be as pious without copying them. The time is imminent to liberate the mind out of their cloaks.

While clerics praise Islam for elevating women's status, educated Muslims know that the worst damage that ever battered women was initiated within the faith. Women before Islam as we will see in details, were not veiled nor forbidden to frequent men or handle business in broad daylight and after dark. The new religion changed all that. It did stop an age old Bedouin practice: the "Wa'ad" or live burial of newborn females (to avoid their taken hostages through frequent inter-tribal raids). But reduced the female inheritance to half the male's share and necessitated two female witnesses against one male in any testimony. The Prophet himself termed his wives who were the crème of the society and "Mothers of Believers", as "lacking intellect and creed . . . man's mind blowers" . . . Women's further restrictive measures have been sadly escalating thanks to the recent radical waves. Many women across the Muslim world endure a difficult impasse: if not chastised by the society for noncompliance, hellfire is the anticipated punishment.

On the other hand western scholars may continue to blame and harass Muslims endlessly. They may break through the working of their minds but fail to see the underlying reasons that inspire their dilemmas. Their knowledge of Islam is generally external and scholastic. In this 21st. century a liberal insight at the depth of this monolithic faith is due. It serves to penetrate the many somber veils that continue to shroud its substance. We see in this attempt a service to both Muslims and Christians in soothing their surging "clash of civilizations."

Perhaps the focal message in this research is to convince Muslims it is high time to boldly renovate their faith from antiquated traditionalism to modern consistencies. We know it would be hard to find among Muslims and many Christians anyone willing to liberate God and the Truth. It is also a rarity to unearth a knowledgeable scholar that hits the absolute truth or a hardy pioneer willing to endanger his life and reveal what he conceals. But Islam could be also a religion of largesse when it comes to interpretations. The old adage that it is good "for any time or place" would not be with a measure of tolerance a trite and deceptive repetition. Muslims should remember—and know if they don't—that the major textual changes in the Koran were inflicted by the third Caliph Othman Bin Affan himself. The purpose was to sustain the emerging requisites of the far-flung conquests and introduce an expedient Islam able to control the vanquished ethnic varieties. Islam today abounds with personalities much more educated than Othman though they may not enjoy his prestigious aura. The faith needs them for updating and refining, including daring textual Koran changes back to initial format to meet today's global co-existence. Failing that Muslims' isolation within their own world and alienation without would continue to ebb and flow endlessly.

Muslim intellectuals should agree as Christian Europe did centuries ago that religions are 0nly made for the service of men. The exact opposite has been going on so far within the Islamic sphere. The time has come for this ongoing servility to stop. It has become crucial for the Muslim mind to embrace openness and clear thinking. What distresses the keen observer is to see Muslim clerics in eternal defense of their religion. They expound it, propagate it and defend it like a political party. Their endless, obstinate struggles take up prime times on major Arab TV screens. By doing so, they inadvertently—and unfortunately—strip Islam and expose it to scrutiny. In fact what is needed is a gallant step like Othman's to free the old, marred scripture from appended mutilations and put it out again in its original version: an adaptation of a Judeo-Christian doctrine suitable to the thinking patterns of the modern Muslim not the old Bedouins of Arabia. The times of advanced technologies differ from the age of tribal raids, camels and horses.

It is also time for modern Muslim clerics to understand that many Koran's intermittent revelations in Medina were circumstantial. They were used to clarify emerging situations, support contingent actions, curse a foe or defend a friend. Muslims should realize those verses had served their purpose 1400 years ago; they should not be applicable nor used on events and peoples of our era. It is also time for them to differentiate between part of the "Nasara" or Nazarene that the Koran revered and recommended, whose dispersed factions in Hijaz were first to embrace Islam and the other "Nasara" Christians whom Muhammad had never met. This knowledge, when vigilantly established shall further appease the ongoing 'clash' and usher in fruitful dialogues.

This book has been written for those exacting scholars, Christians and Muslims alike, who crave credible outlooks on the inception and proliferation of Islam. We request readers to focus their moral fiber not disgruntled spirit on the basic historical and social realities they are about to discover. The plain truth and the logical not the prosaic version is what they will go through in the following pages. Every statement has been researched down to its core. References and referrals are recorded to please and pacify the perceptive mind. We know a monumental scholastic upheaval will ensue as a result. Appraising a tumultuous, 1400 years old faith is a daring process that will wake and shake many minds and spirits.

THREE

Mecca and Young Muhammad

"Mecca's length from the west is 78 degrees, its width 23 degrees. It is said to be situated 21 points under the tropic of Cancer. Its lucky star is Taurus and is located in the second province of Arabia."

Ptolemy

"He who endures Mecca's heat for one hour, would be distant a 100-year walk from Hell, and 200-year stride to Paradise."

Muhammad

Mecca, the birthplace of Muhammad, was a desolate town deprived of any desert shrubs or even hardy date trees. A canyon between somber, scorched mountains that survives on limited drinking water and meager resources. Its long, agonizing summer heat and the scarcity of its life-supporting means branded Mecca as one the bleakest spot in the old world for the living of man. The town's setting is uninviting: the earth is dry and dusty and smolders under a relentless sun; the whole region is scoured by hot, throbbing desert winds. Although sometimes rain does not fall for years when it does come it can be heavy, creating torrents of water that rush down from the hills and flood the desiccated basin grounds of the town where it is swiftly guzzled in. As a backdrop for divine revelation the area is every bit as fitting as the mountains of Sinai or the wilderness of Judea.

This seemingly disenchanted town was in those days the unchallenged capital of the major part of Arabia—what loosely constitutes the Arabian Peninsula today for three main reasons:

1- The geographical position:

Arabia was divided into two regions: the arid area of the north and the rain-fed area of the south. The southern region of Yemen and Oman was blessed with resources of soil and climate. Because of its fertile land and strategic location on the commerce routes the south had enjoyed a developed form of political life and advanced culture. As a confederation of states the region was heavily populated and governed by different kingdoms at different times. It was as a result greatly influenced by foreign cultures and religions such as Christianity, Zoroastrianism and Judaism. Most of the southern peoples were not Arabs, but Sabians or Himyarites of Semitic descent who spoke a Semitic language of their own.

The northern region on the other hand was inhabited primarily by two groups: the Bedouins and the settled tribes. The Bedouins were tough nomadic shepherds constantly on the move. On the outskirts of the deserts there was a ring of oases where the tribes had settled. Most of the important settlements were in western Arabia, such as Najran, Mecca, Yathrib (Medina) and Taif. The settled tribes relied on agriculture or commerce for their livelihood. Their spoken language was Arabic. The inhabitants of the north and south were constantly interacting with each other. There were Arabs who lived in the south and there were Sabian communities in the north. In fact it was the south that helped urbanize the north-west by opening up the deserts to trade and shifting the world commerce route to western Arabia which created the caravan cities and the communities of traders.

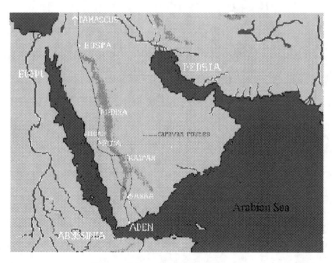

The old caravans routes

In old Arabia where moving goods and people inland depended solely on camel caravans selected stopovers were established to break long journeys, recuperate and provision in preparation for the next long ones. Mecca was gifted with a unique position being midway between Aden, the metropolis of southern Arabia and Damascus, the enormous consumer market of Syria. It was also a commercial destination for traders arriving by ships from Oman to deposit through nearby Jeddah port their much needed Indian spices for further distribution in the peninsula at large.

Neighboring towns would flock into Mecca for a double purpose: perform pilgrimage to the Holy Site and secure their provisions. The adage "hajja'w hijja": "pilgrimage and purpose" is still a statement for modern day pilgrims. Mecca's merchants basked in unprecedented wealth and prestige. The town's religious cachet further enhanced its stature. It was soon called Um-ul-Qura: "the mother of towns", a nickname that continued through history until this day. H. Gibb, professor of Arabic at Oxford University further comments: "Mecca at this time was no sleepy hollow remote from the noise and bustle of the world. A busy and wealthy commercial town, almost monopolizing the entrepot trade between the Indian Ocean and the Mediterranean, it recalls Palmyra without the flashy Greek veneer. Its citizens, while preserving a certain native Arab simplicity, acquired a wide knowledge of people and cities in their intercourse, commercial and diplomatic, with Arab tribesmen and Roman officials. Amongst their leaders these experiences had stimulated intellectual faculties and moral qualities of prudence and self-restraint rare in Arabia".

2- The religious site:

The Qaaba where today's Muslims are required to face five times every day for prayers is thought to have been the original house of worship constructed of stone blocks by Prophet Abraham and his son Ismael although the Bible doesn't mention any of that. Yet tradition has it that it was erected on the original site of a sanctuary established by the "first Prophet", Adam, after his expulsion from Paradise. Embedded in the corner of the structure is the Black Stone, a seemingly small meteorite block used by Abraham as a foundation stone.

Over the years Abraham's message was forgotten for lack of assimilation. As Mecca became increasingly prosperous in the sixth century A.D. pagan idols of varying sizes and shapes proliferated. By the early seventh century a pantheon of some 360 statues and icons adorned the Qaaba's interior including a primitive rendering of Jesus and the Virgin Mary. Idolatrous tribes to whom Judaism and Christianity were too idiomatic to penetrate continued to perform the Mecca pilgrimage. The Black Stone carried a special sanctity status: it has always been worshipped as the "Greatest Idol" of Quraish, the largest and most influential pre-Islamic tribal jamboree in southern Arabia and the traditional custodian of the Shrine. Yearly pilgrimage to the Qaaba to worship the idols and touch the Holy Stone picked up unrelenting. It became an important business enterprise to Quraish and further confirmed its supremacy in the peninsula. The two main commodities offered were: Yemeni/Damascene goods . . . and drinking water!

In the rest of Arabia the situation was bleak. For centuries the Bedouin tribes of the regions of Hijaz and Najd had lived in fierce competition with one another for the basic necessities of life. To help people cultivate the communal spirit that was essential for survival the Arabs had evolved an ideology called "muruwah" (manliness, courage, endurance) which fulfilled many of the functions of religion. In the conventional sense the Arabs had little time for religion. There was a pagan pantheon of deities including al-Lat, the High God and the Izza. Arabs worshipped at their dispersed shrines in addition to the great black stone of Qaaba but did not develop a mythology that explained the relevance of these gods and holy places to the spiritual life. They had no notion of an afterlife but believed instead that *Kadar, or* "fate," was supreme—an attitude that was probably essential in a society where the mortality rate was so high.

Drinking water, the basic life sustenance was not obtainable all the time. A Bedouin as his camel may not drink water when he wanted but only when it is available. The famous Jewish Arabian poet Samow'al (Samuel,) prided himself over all Arabs in one of his poems of what his father Adiya did to him:

"Adiya built me a citadel, fortified and outfitted
With a well, so I could drink whenever I desired . . ."

Even later in Islam ablution using clean sand was in order in the absence of water.

Mecca was also a center for Christianity; an overlooked fact that surprises many historians. This faith however did not flourish in the Arabian Peninsula for one obvious reason: most of the people were illiterate. As it requires lots of manuscripts and directives to read and practice it was confined to the little elite that could decipher primordial Arabic and Aramaic writing. This has caused much distress to Bishop Waraka head of the Mecca church who worked hard and in vain for its proliferation. His full legacy and blueprints in establishing a simplified Judeo/Christian faith that turned out later to be Islam are detailed in the following pages.

3- The commercial center:

Mecca could not rely solely on the meager revenues of the poor tribal pilgrims or the local sales of goods for its prosperity. Entrepreneurial and dynamic Quraish soon discovered the vast advantages of travel and trade and established early in the 6th. Century several caravan trips to the two prominent commercial centers of the region: Damascus and Aden. The two main movements were dubbed "the winter and summer trips". As soon as heat starts simmering, half of Mecca's male population would set out atop thousands of camels destined to Damascus. They sell and barter their light but valuable camel loads of Yemeni incense and Indian spices as main articles of trade then reload their "desert ships" with Damascene products of brassware, silks, nuts, grains and dried fruits.

Throughout the long, one-month journey, poetry is composed during the day's march inspired by the camels' cadenced steps to be recited later in the evening amid a circling array of light tents and ruminating camels. One major midway stop in this journey for exhausted men and emaciated animals was the Busra Convent where vicar Bahira a subordinate of Bishop Waraka would open his domain and provide hospitality to the weary traders, receive the Bishop's mailed instructions and send back his reports. About half the Damascene goods would later find their way to Yemen over the winter caravan. The other half is split between sales to the Qaaba pilgrims and local consumption.

The tremendous wealth and power were unfortunately enjoyed by the controlling cluster of Quraish's nobility. The majority of the Mecca populace vacillates in sheer poverty and depravation; a typical have-and-have-not society. Quraish's tycoons in a further step to protect their immense fortunes and keep the hungry wolves at bay employed thousands of Africans, mostly Abyssinians as camel herders, handymen and even armed forces when need calls. The tribal pride dearer to an Arab than his own soul, was inhibitive. He would prefer to rather die from hunger than dole out for one of his tribe's masters. While hospitality was readily acceptable within kinship, foods and similar aids were categorically refused and begging for help even by insinuation was the most dishonorable act. In the shadow of the apparent Meccan prosperity constant famine struck so hard the needy majority to the point of—i'itifad—or "self-afflicted hunger death". Historian Muhammad bin Anas states: "When hunger walloped them severely and hopelessly they used to close their doors on them, wrap their bodies with branches and stoically quiver to death."

Muhammad, the orphan of a destitute family spent his miserable early years in bone-dry Mecca unlike any other normal child.

His father Abdullah died shortly before he was born. His mother Amina was so distressed by the tragic loss of her husband and sole supporter that milk dried in her breasts. She carried the newborn to Thowaiba, the maid of Abu Lahab, who breast fed him for few days. The same woman happened to have fed much earlier his famous uncle Hamza who would grow to become a respected and arduous knight in Quraish. Thowaiba then delivered the baby to Halima, a Bedouin woman outside Mecca to feed him with her son Abdullah for two more years. Historians omitted who nurtured Muhammad until he was six when 'he was given back to his mother', who 'took him to Medina to visit the tombs of his father and uncles'. Amina died shortly (576BC) when the boy was hardly eight. A lady friend of hers, Um Ayman, took him to his grandfather Abdul Mutalib who cared for him until he died three years later. He was then moved to the custody of his uncle Abu Talib, who already had a younger kid, Ali, destined to become later the dean of all Shia sects.

Muhammad's youth witnessed three nursing mothers in addition to his own and two caring men plus three 'milk-brothers' including his uncle Hamza.

Historians agree that Abu Taleb used to bestow on his young nephew a mixture of excessive zeal and anxiety. He was always "mindful of a harming hand or a hideous event and was thus alert to calculate any negative happening. He would often draw the boy from his bed and replace him by his son Ali to make sure of his well being and dissipate his own intense anxiety about him." "Abu Taleb could not bear being away from Muhammad. Even when his duty called on the Damascus caravans he would keep him in his company irrespective of how the young boy would endure the trip." (Sulaiman Ketani-historian).

What was the reason behind this intense preoccupation of the uncle towards his nephew? Was Muhammad suffering an unusual ailment? Was it the intense containment or a mixture of negative feelings of orphanage and destitution? Abu Taleb used to notice the loneliness and seclusion of young Muhammad and his need to lift his spirit out of lingering depression. Could it be the successive bereavements of his parents and grandfather that intensified his bitter solitude or his rancor against the cruel fate and the callous society?

The boy was suffering ruthless conditions of emotional distress, anxiety, apprehension and communal alienation. The social fiber of Mecca was invaded by all sorts of conflicting political and dogmatic currents, crammed with money moguls, business magnets and consumers. He saw with his own eyes huge funds and commodities changing hands among the wealthy Yemenis, Damascenes and Meccans while his impoverished class plummets deeper in poverty and depression. He saw the inhabitants of 'the high society quarter' eating in gold plates, living in 'the high above' apartments, wearing the Damascene velvet and the Yemen silky garments, 'they sleep on elevated beds', their mattresses are 'stuffed and puffy' and their 'divans mellifluous'. They whip the assets of the orphans and the penniless. Those who owed money were forced to prostitute their women and daughters in repayment . . .

These were the 'feeble' that constitute the majority of Mecca's populace; Muhammad could not bear looking at them. Those were branded by the tyrants in various names: 'the scrawny gang', 'the Arab wolves', 'the desert thieves' and 'the bad hordes'. Their food derived from tree leaves, grass, wild shrubs and animals. They would even break the stripped-off bones and cook their marrows . . .

The picture is bleak. Hunger eats the hearts of those who refused to beg or solicit. It penetrates their houses to devour them. The crisis grows to dreadful dimensions. Muhammad is terrified. His kinfolks "smell awful for lack of washing, lice mess about their hair and move freely over their bodies" (Jawad Ali, historian). He is perplexed with no apparent solution in his hand. Abu Taleb reads his predicament yet fears his nephew was not simply disgruntled by his living circumstances but in the throes of a wayward physical or mental condition thus, "he could not bear being away from him".

Was Muhammad slightly epileptic? The convulsions he would go through intermittently could have been the symptoms. In modern day diagnostics these were 'moderate psychomotor attacks during which a patient acts withdrawn and behaves strangely for a few minutes and sometimes roams around or tugs at his clothes'. (Ernest Rodin, psychiatrist). This was apparent in the intermittent convulsions recurred later through his manhood most probably under the spasms of revelations as his young wife Aisha was quoted saying: "when revelation comes a convulsion would seize him and he would ask to be covered. Droplets of water would show on his front." She also said: "Harith Ibn Hesham asked the messenger of Allah: "how do you receive the revelation?" "Sometimes it comes to me like a ringing bell and this is the hardest. When he (Gabriel) leaves me I remember what he said" Muhammad answered. Then he continued, "Sometimes the angel appears to me as a man; he speaks to me and I remember what he said." Aisha confirmed later what his first wife Khadija experienced earlier when she said, "I saw him when revelation comes down to him: sweat covers his forehead in the very cold day."

In fact many 'feeble' in Mecca suffered such intensive torments; ailments varying between psychopathic, epilepsy, nervous breakdown or even hysteria. It is unimaginable what would happen to the human mind when a need-constrained man delivers his wife or daughter to perversion or induce self-death by hunger. Such convulsions grew up and continued to lash Muhammad through manhood especially later under the strenuous regimen of spiritual meditations.

It is apparent that Muhammad, one of the most controversial persons in the history of mankind, was born, lived and died as a genius who endured extreme suffering. When he reached his teens he accompanied Abu Taleb and was close to him through his Damascus trips as a guard to Quraish's caravans. He wanted him to stand on his feet and earn his living. Many times he would tell him: 'my nephew, I am a penniless man, we have no trade or life sustenance.' (Ibn Saad, historian). Those frequent trips to Damascus helped the young man get rid of his Mecca's gloomy surroundings but did not rid him of that melancholically wrapping shroud; an alienation that haunted him throughout his future life. He could not mend his disrupted emotional ties with the society.

His sexual drive started erupting beyond gratification. The pretty girls in Mecca and Damascus were unreachable stars. It was a kind of developmental alienation that rendered him disoriented and withdrawn; a silent revolt ensued within him rejecting all values of his discriminating society.

The vague Christian faith practiced by his uncle and many of his clans under Bishop Waraka was not within his grasp. Through his strolls around the Qaaba the funny statues of meaningless idols did not stir him except for one: the picture of Mary and baby Jesus. He already heard his uncle repeatedly saying they belong to 'the people of the Book'. He wished one day to be able to understand that Book.

Muhammad's 'cosmic alienation' however took a positive turn while approaching his twenties. Two Christian chieftains: Waraka the Bishop of Mecca and Abu Bakr the young business tycoon saw in him a promising talent for leadership. They decided to initiate him into the realm of general knowledge and the fine art of eloquence. For this purpose they would send him back to the desert to live with his foster mother Halima at Bani Saad dwellings to interact with the Bedouins along with his foster brother and develop the pure and correct forms of expressions. On one of the Damascene trips Muhammad and his uncle were received in a private audience in Busra by vicar Bahira. This visit was not a coincidence. It was carefully arranged by Waraka for an important purpose.

Bahira was the vicar of Busra's convent, "he lived there in the second half of the sixth century. He used to preach Bedouins to adopt the monolith faith. Caravans' tenders regularly stopped over at Bahira's; where he would offer them plenty of food." (Sira Halabia, history). During that meeting Bahira was impressed by Muhammad. A story has it that the monk asked the young man to bare his back, when he did so Bahira looked for and delightfully found a dark mole by the left shoulder. He then displayed a broad smile and told Abu Taleb: behold, this is the prophet of this nation! Another story simply stated that Bahira advised Muhammad that 'a bright future' is in the offing and 'warned Abu Taleb to protect him from the Jews.' The two stories, disseminated among the tenders, had one purpose: Muhammad started being prepared for the big task ahead!

FOUR

Uproars in the Peninsula

"If it wasn't to Islam, Tagleb would have eaten the people"

Caliph Omar bin Al-Khattab

The Sixth century started in Arabia with two major uproars that fermented together to produce the Islamic faith:

1/ after expulsing with help from Constantinople of the two rival tribes Khoza'a and Bakr at the turn of the century, chieftain Qusay became the sole master of

Mecca. He merged under his leadership the dispersed small tribes and gave the name Quraish—or mixture—to the new integration. Qusay became a wealthy man; he consolidated in his hands the total custody over Qaaba including: the custodianship, the keys, the Consultative House, the flag, the pilgrims' catering and most importantly: the drinking water. Two of his sons begot Assad and Hashem. Assad begot Nofal, the father of Waraka and Khowiled, father of Khadija the future wife of the Prophet. On the other hand Hashem begot Abdul Mutaleb who in turn begot Abdullah, Muhammad's father and Abu Taleb, his uncle, custodian and Ali's father.

Our concern from this chronology is to establish that our main four players: Waraka, Khadija, Muhammad and Ali, all derived from the same patriarch Qusai. They together share a pure and prestigious Arabian legacy unparalleled in all Quraish. Qusai was the first to rebuild the Qaaba, recuperate and reposition its pilfered corner Black Stone and roof it with timbers; also the first to remove tents and build stone houses. Fate ordained though that Waraka and Khadija belonged to the haves, Muhammad and Ali to the have-nots. By their same relationship to Qusai however, both the bishop and the prophet-to-be had the same source of pride and prestige.

2/ Mecca's power and prosperity expanded throughout Arabia yet it did not go unchallenged. The Christian tribe of Tagleb who ruled the fertile land stretching from Najran down to the Red Sea and from Asir to Yemen started threatening Mecca's interests. Its people were so laborious and organized they transformed their mountainous land into stretches of terraced gardens sustained with abundant water resources. Christian Tagleb became in the south, like Jewish Khyber in the north, a bread basket for hungry Arabia.

When their capital Najran started as a new hob for caravans Quraish sensed the looming danger. Before feeling the pinch Mecca's tycoons convened in the Consultative House to discuss their fortunes and prepare strategies to face Tagleb. Abu Bakr, the Christian mogul, maintained that the enemy may be vanquished at war but it would be a costly one splitting the rest of the Arabs. He added that Tagleb is well regarded by others because they have a religion and a Kitab (book); here in Mecca they still worship hollow and vague deities that many poets in the peninsula started ridiculing. Contradicting opinions clamored in the House: all Arabs are now pilgrims to the Shrine; who would risk losing such a lucrative business? Abu Bakr assured fellow members the pilgrimage ritual was essentially to the Shrine of Abraham not Habal (Quraish's idol) and will ever remain so and that he had something in the pump; all he needed was time.

Historians who missed out knowingly or inadvertently on these debates and their essential substance should perhaps review what the third Caliph Omar said later: 'If it wasn't to Islam, Tagleb would have eaten the people!'

At the time those uproars engulfed Arabia another religious movement would soon change the fate of all Arabs; a great labor of a 'skillful erudite' was slowly but steadily inscribed on scrolls: Bishop Waraka's works.

FIVE

Ebionism

"Theirs was seclusion, devoutness and piousness for long nights . . . and practicing good deeds . . ."

Ibn Hisham—Historian

P alestine witnessed before the appearance of Jesus, throughout his ministry and up till the destruction of the Temple a revival of two major spiritual movements led by Jewish "Ebionim" (Poor). The first was pioneered by the Torah's "truth-seekers", those who believed in intense solitary meditation conducive to the penetration of the inner human soul and healing human ailments through that process. The second were followers of the Christian mystique faith; the version variably ministered by Jesus not his Jerusalem disciples but certainly by Paul. Both movements selected for their pious retreats scattered caves in the Qumran Mountain near the Dead Sea where the famous "Scrolls" were recently discovered.

Along with the two main sects or schools of Judaism: Pharisees and Sadducees, the Essenes and Ebionites were reticent, low profile movements made up of mostly Jewish/Israelite that were dispersed in Palestine and the eastern regions above the Dead Sea. This is where they led a Sufi, mystique life of prayers and contemplation within a school of puritan spirituality based on the biblical teachings.

The earlier wave of Ebionites totally withdrew from the alluring world to the dreary solitude of Sufism. Using the Bible's austere principles they developed their rigorous regimen of mastering the soul through its inner depth or what we call the subconscious mind today. This mastery, sustained by thorough abandonment of worldly desires and intense development of the spirit achieved for them the superiority of mind over matter and soul over body. A school that produced two brilliant disciples and of them changed the course of humanity: John the Baptist and Jesus Christ.

The Scripture hardly mentions Jesus' "known years", from birthday to age 12 and from 30 to Resurrection; the "lost 18 years" in between vanished into oblivion. Yet the Baptist who shared Jesus the same "lost years" bluntly displayed his Ebionite upbringing and way of life: a tough desert man who went "in all the region round about Jordan" wearing "a raiment of camel's hair and a leathern girdle about his loins, feeding on locust and wild honey and preaching in the wilderness of Judea that the kingdom of heaven is at hand". In heralding Jesus, John epitomized Isaiah's prophecy to "prepare the way of the Lord and make his path straight". This merciless and controversial forerunner who harshly called the Pharisees and Sadducees "a generation of vipers" announced Jesus as: "he that comes after me was mightier than I, whose shoe strings I am not worthy to unloose". He certainly "knew" the spiritual powers of Jesus. He would not know that hadn't he also spent his "lost years" in the company of the Master "round about Jordan!"

The Essenes or "Doers of Torah" who wrote the Dead Sea Scrolls pioneered certain aspects of this "Way" over 150 years before the birth of Jesus. They were a wilderness, baptizing, new covenant, messianic/apocalyptic group expecting a redemptive Figure: the Messiah. They saw themselves as the remnant core of God's faithful people preparing the Way for the return of His Glory. Like Ebionites they too referred to themselves as the Way, the Poor, the Saints, the Children of Light and so forth. Perhaps their most common trait was the brotherhood or cluster and they referred to themselves as brothers and sisters. They were bitterly opposed to the corrupt Priests in Jerusalem and even to the Pharisees whom they saw as compromising with the occupying Roman powers. They had their own ideals and developed aspects which Jesus picks up. They followed one "True Teacher", the Teacher of Righteousness that dwells *in the human mind*; a philosophy that later constituted the core of the Jesus ministry modified and disseminated through his powerful, prophetic influence as Teacher.

Most of the Ebionite doctrine's features were anticipated in the teachings of the earlier Qumran sect as revealed in the **Dead Sea Scrolls**. They believed in one God and taught that Jesus was the Messiah and was the true "prophet" mentioned in Deuteronomy 18:15. The Ebionites believed Jesus became the Messiah because he obeyed the Mosaic Law. They themselves faithfully followed the Law although they removed what they regarded as interpolations in order to uphold their teachings which included vegetarianism, holy poverty, ritual ablutions, and the rejection of animal sacrifices.

Ebionites formed a two-fold sect: while others did not make the distinction some scholars considered that Eusebius and Origen were confusing them with another group called the **Nazarenes**. It has not been established whether the Nazarenes or the Ebionites were the "true Christians" who became later according to Islam the "true Muslims" wordhipping Allah. Not only that the Koran did say specifically that "the real believers will prevail" but it seems that neither the Nazarenes (even if they were heretics) nor the Ebionites ever prevailed later against the rest of the Pauline orthodox Christianity.

The Ebionites main beliefs:

-   One God and one God only; they do not accept Jesus as God.
-   Follow the gospel of Matthew only (a different version than the one found in the New Testament).
-   They reject Paul, though he visited them in Qumran by instructions of Hanania the Damascene after Jesus'

miraculous appearance to him, and considered him a
renegade, intruder and an apostate from the Law.
- They observe the Sabbath.
- They hold the observance of the Mosaic Law (the
corrected version introduced by Jesus) as necessary for
salvation.
- They maintain that Jesus is a mere man who had to
merit his title, Son of God, by fulfilling the Law.
- Jesus came to do away with animal sacrifices.
- They renounce all riches and give up all goods and
possessions.
- They admit Abraham, Isaac, Jacob, Moses, Aaron,
Joshua, but none of the prophets (David, Solomon,
Isaiah, Jeremiah, Daniel, Ezekiel, Elijah, Elisha). They
believe that Jesus alone is the true prophet.

A doctrinal battle raged after the death of Jesus between
their Original Apostles based in Jerusalem and Paul over
primarily (but not exclusively) the deification of Jesus. They
sent out emissaries to Paul's churches telling them that he is
teaching a false doctrine (Paul's letters are primarily aimed at
countering these visits.) The "So called special apostles" (2
Cor 11:5) that Paul defended himself against were none other
than the original Ebionite apostles: Peter, John and James
the "brother" of Jesus. They *almost* prevailed. Paul himself
admits that his followers are leaving him: "All deserted me"
[2 Tim 4:16]. Even his closest friends Barnabas and Demas,
(2Tim 4:10 and Gal 2:13) returned to the side of the Original
Apostles.

But the Romans reconquered Jerusalm and expulsed the Ebionites with much of the Jewish population out into the desert. This event helped Paul's version to become accepted among his churches.

Most Ebionites of Qumran followed and supported Jesus throughout his 3-year ministry and established the "Church of Jerusalem" after his resurrection. They accepted their modified version of the Gospel according to Mathew only. They called it "the Gospel according to the Hebrews'. They copied it roughly but sparingly from the same Aramaic Mathew Gospel which was in their opinion unoriginal and incomplete. This was later confirmed by Epiphanos, the bishop of Cyprus. The Church of Jerusalem moved again with its monks to the Qumran convent much before the destruction of the Temple in the year 70AD. Those monks resumed Christ's teachings in their secluded enclave. They migrated later to Western Arabia or Hijaz and rallied around them few Arabian tribes who embraced the faith distantly up till the sixth century. Bishop Waraka and his assistant Bahira were two of their staunchest advocates.

To sum it up, the Ebionite remnants were Christened Jews who believed Jesus and saw in Him another great prophet. They did not recognize His deity and attached his status as the son of God to his executing the Law. They believed he was a great man who was inspired after his baptism by John the Baptist. His message was that of preaching and enlightenment but not redemption and deliverance. They trusted solely the word of 'the Son of Miriam' and chose Jerusalem as their aspiration light in prayers which in fact remained the beacon for Muhammad well after announcing Islam. "He reverted to Mecca after Waraka's death and migration to Medina where rebuttal by Jews to his doctrine became apparent." (Asad Rustom—historian).

Ebionism encompasses almost all the specific traits of the early Judeo-Nazarene faith that preceded the 'Apostolic Church' founded later by Paul. Those traits are closely incorporated in Islam. Items:

1/ **The Christ:** Jesus is a prophet superior to any other prophet as "He is embedded with an angelic spirit". (Tertullien-theologian). He was not a Messiah in the beginning; he became one later at baptism. He was "born and created by the God Father and is the first Archangel". They do believe that "Messiah was integrated with Jesus the day of his baptism at the Jordan River and left him the day he was martyred". So Jesus "was crucified shortly after the Messiah left him". They also believe Jesus had the capability to transmute into any personage as he frequently vanished from his arraigners' sight. He had the power to raise the dead, heal the sick and 'convert clay into a bird.' Exactly the same descriptions reverberate in the Koran.

2/ **Mary:** Ebionites believe all what Mathew said about Mary in his gospel. From her prestigious lineage to Jacob, to her miraculous birth, to her entering the Temple at three and being fed by the angel of God, down to the Annunciation, the holy Conception and the glorious birth of Christ. The Koran repeats patchily the same attributes.

3/ **The Holy Spirit:** exactly as in Judaism and Christianity revelation either came from God or through His angels.

It was confused between the two exactly as in the Old and New Testaments, examples: "and the angel of the Lord came up and said, I made you to go out of Egypt etc . . ." (Judges 2/1); was it the angel who did what he said or God who did. Or, "and the angel of the Lord spoke to Philip saying, arise and go toward the South etc . . . (Acts 8/26). Here again, the angel of God /the Holy Spirit who said. Was the angel of God in these and many similar texts a separate personality or was it God Himself? The same confusion appears in the Koran between Archangel Gabriel and the Holy Spirit: "Say, whoever is the enemy to Gabriel—for he (Gabriel) brings down the revelation to your heart". (Koran 2/97). And:" Say, the Holy Spirit has brought down the revelation from your Lord in truth". (Koran 16/102).

4/ **Circumcision**: This old practice dating back to ancient Pharaohs and continued through history in Africa and Arabia involving both sexes was further reinforced on males in the Bible to distinguish the Hebrews. Christianity and Islam did not delineate for it being an accepted tradition. Prophet Muhammad though included women in his *Hadith*: "circumcision is a rule for men and a distinction for women"; and another while passing by a woman circumciser: "do not spare but be fair". Early Christians and certainly Ebionite practiced male circumcision until Apostle Paul revoked it altogether.

5/ **Ablution and cleansing** were routine practices to Nazarenes and Ebionite in line with the Torah's instructions. 'Washing for them was a daily task before meals, prayers or after sexual insemination.' Islam adopted the same scheme but distinguished between the major wash for the whole body and the minor ablution involving face, hands and feet only. In the absence of water clean sand would be an acceptable substitute.

6/ **Wine prohibition** took early roots among Nazarenes and Ebionites but not Hebrews and Christians. Ebionites disallowed even mixing bread offering with wine and used fresh water instead. Islam applied the same principle and denounced wine on earth as "an abomination—of Satan's handiwork". (Koran 5/90). In paradise however Islam promised: "Rivers of wine, a joy to those who drink". (Koran 47/15). Muhammad further described the paradise wine as "white as milk". At his times the famous transparent Arak of Lebanon and Syria that turns milky with added water was as is still today the delightful alcoholic drink.

7/ **Pork meat prohibition** was imposed by Judaism: "and the swine, though he divides the hoof . . . their flesh shall you not eat . . . they are unclean to you". (Levit.11/8). Ebionites and Nazarenes followed the same rule while Christians dropped all food distinctions: only man renders food clean or unclean. The Koran reverted to the early Moses doctrine and followed the Judeo-Nazarene traditions declaring: "He has only forbidden you dead meat and the blood and the flesh of swine . . ." (Koran 2/173). This formal prohibition is mentioned repeatedly.

8/ **Fasting** is a shared command among all faiths. In Islam it follows the same instruction drawn by the

Judeo-Nazarenes: "the fasting day starts when one can distinguish the white thread from the blue one" (Talmud 1/5). The Koran follows the same distinction: ". . . eat and drink until the white thread at dawn appears to you distinct from the black thread . . ." (Koran 2/187).

In these and many other religious aspects we see striking resemblance between Ebionism and Islam such as women, marriage and divorce, prayer, offering, and most importantly social assistance and welfare.

SIX

Waraka's Works

"God distinguished us above all. We are the masters and leaders of the Arabs."

Bishop Waraka

Waraka relates as we have seen to one of the best embedded and respected branch of Quraish with direct lineage to Qusai its original patriarch. His reputable ancestry was closely shared by Abu Taleb, Khadija, Muhammad and Ali. In those days noble ethnic belonging is a criterion in determining the person's status and merits. It is the same to this day in many societies.

Bishop Waraka's Ebionite Christianity has been an absolute certainty to historians. He was known to have mastered the two foreign languages spoken by Jesus Christ: Hebrew and Aramaic. Arabic was not simply his mother tongue, he was an authority in this language as well as a high ranked poet. In those days of illiteracy gifted poets were what the media is today. To 'own' a poet then was for rulers and Caliphs similar in social and political importance to launching a T.V. station or a newspaper today. Arabic poetry singles itself among many other languages with poems exceeding a thousand verses having the same rhyme and rhythm. Poetry, easy to commit to memory, was called rightfully the 'Documentary of the Arabs.' Its twin but no less equal in importance was the oratory eloquence. This dignified art had two rivaling princes at that time: Waraka bin Nofal of Mecca and Bin Saida Ayadi the Nestorian Bishop of Tagleb in Najran. Besides outclassing others in these two noble arts historians distinguished Waraka as was "well versed in Christianity; he studied the books from their origins and taught faith to the 'People of the Book." (Ibn Hisham-historian).

The many Jewish-Nazarene groups living around Mecca and Hijaz had contradicting dogmas that thrived pointlessly at the time. Jewish tribes had lived in Arabia for hundreds of years by the time Muhammad was born. They were well established, prosperous and highly respected. Among the Nazarenes there were the Ebionite who denied the deity of Christ; the Diocetic Gnostic who emphasized His deity but denied His humanity; the Arians who attributed to Him a subordinate deity and the Nestorians who denied the proper union of His two natures. There were also Elxaism and Cerinthism, who advocated a paradise full of sensual delights. The Koran mentioned these factions repeatedly: 'and the (Nazarene) parties disagreed among themselves' (Koran—19/28), and, 'some of the (Nazarene) parties who denounce each other' (Koran—13/26). The best known of these 'parties' were the Ebionite to whom Waraka was affiliated. He was a Nazarene Ebionite from tip to toe. He loathed the long and inconclusive debates over the twin-nature of Christ. He did not believe Christ to be 'the Son of God, equal to Him in essence' and could not unfathom Jesus' elevation of men from from "the slave of God" to the "son of God".

Waraka was also a follower of another Nazarene: Cerinth who advocated that the role of Christ was to liberate his people from the Roman domination; thus it was a socio-political move through enlightenment and redemption. And the heavenly kingdom of Christ is very much similar to many places on earth. Cerinth also believed heavenly Paradise to be a haven for all human joys and ecstasies: its delights are there for the total bliss of the human body including food, drinks and most importantly sexual pleasures. The Islamic Janna 'Paradise' reflects Cerinth's envisioning with all the garnishing a Bedouin craves: 'Gardens with rivers of wine, milk and honey flowing underneath and fair maidens with lovely eyes'. The plain controversy in Waraka's thinking is that he was torn between the rigid Ebionite Puritanism advocated for man's living on earth and the loose Cerinthic sensualities men will be rewarded after death. That led him to deliver a blended package of Ebionite spiritual abstinence as well as Cerinthic sexual indulgence in worldly life; with another Janna's delicacies for the promised few . . .

Bishop Waraka represented explicitly the Arab brain that assimilates only the palpable and blatant and avoids theorizing and dwelling into details. Ebionism to him was the best form of simplified Christian faith: Christ was not God but a great prophet. He was not crucified but a look-alike was. Both Torah and Gospel should be implemented. Helping the poor and attributing delights to Paradise were all Ebionite traits that Waraka believed in and spent his lifetime promulgating. "They feature fasting one whole month in the year, feeding the poor, consoling the disheartened, denouncing idols and refraining from eating slaughtered offerings, circumcision, washing seminal viscidity, confine oneself to meditation and reading the holy scriptures" (Lisanol—Arab History).

To further adhere to the early practice of the Qumran clerics Waraka selected a grotto in the Nour Mountain East of Mecca called 'the Cave of Hira' where he used to perform his spiritual devotions and contemplations. The Cave—or Ghar—was the secluded Church of Mecca where the Bishop was joined by many zealots including Abdul Mutalib, Howairith, Bin Jahsh, Bin Mughira, and later Abu Bakr, Salman Al Farsi (the Persian) and Muhammad who were the three first pillars of the new religion.

'Waraka was immersed in writing the Hebrew book "the Gospel according to Hebrews" in Arabic. 'He would transcribe the Gospel from Hebrew in whatever God permits' (Sahih, Albukhari-historian). And "he was *writing the Arabic Book* and transcribing from the Gospel into Arabic whatever God permits" (Sahih, Moslem—the most trusted Islamic scholar).

Entrance to Ghar Hira

Many historians who traced Waraka's legacy agreed on his major occupation: he was intent on writing the 'Gospel according to Hebrews' in an Arabic language inspiring piousness and rhymed to invoke easy memorization. Waraka, the poet par excellence, visualized that illiterate Arabs can only commit to memory rhymed poetic sentences as they do poems. Arabs to this day rarely retain texts that are not rhymed or rhythmic. His writing style came midway between poetry and prose; a poetic prose that has a double purpose: commitment to memory and chanted recitation. With this style, Arabs experienced a sense of transcendence: an ultimate reality and power that lie behind the transient and fleeting phenomena of the mundane world. The early biographers of Muhammad constantly described the wonder and shock felt by the Arabs when they heard the Koran for the first time. Many were converted on the spot believing that God alone could account for the extraordinary beauty of the language. Frequently a convert would describe the experience as a divine invasion that tapped buried yearnings and released floods of feelings.

Waraka was distressed to see his Nazarene Christianity losing ground in Arabia let alone within Quraish itself. He would look with jealousy at the Jews and other Christians who had a book in their hands they could read. He would call them 'the People of the Book'. Hence his lifelong preoccupation was to create one that can be read in plain Arabic for which he devised a unique name: the Koran or 'the Readable'—from the Aramaic verb Kara'a or read. As his mind-numbing work approached fruition old Waraka was on the lookout for a bright and personable disciple to learn, sermonize and edify. Muhammad was the ideal candidate.

Waraka was the 'Reyes' of the church and the leader of all Arab Nazarenes. So would be Muhammad the Head (Imam) of all Muslims. "Thus I was ordered and I am the first of Muslims" (Koran, Anaam). To Waraka, Islam (literally: Submission) started with Abraham up to Moses and Jesus. The repetitive referrals to all preceding monolithic prophets were to assert that the Islam of the "skillful erudite" encompasses old faiths in addition to the new one.

The exact date of the Bishop's death was not recorded. It is agreed however that he expired in the 'Year of Sorrow' along with Abu Taleb and Khadija. Islamic historians ignored his whereabouts to bestow on Muhammad and the Revelation the total credit especially that Waraka died on the seventh year of the Islamic Mission. According to a 'Fatwa' he died as a non-Muslim at a time Islam was declared therefore a non-believer; hence his total distancing by historians. Muhammad however rushed to his defense: 'Do not scorn Waraka, I saw him in one or two paradises because he believed and trusted me' and 'I saw Waraka in paradise wearing silken clothes' (Sira, history). The Prophet wanted to ascertain here that although he died as a non-Muslim he was elevated to the high paradise. Waraka did not publicly embrace the new religion at his old age of 99 when he became blind and hard of hearing. In fact he did not have to: the Ebionite Islam was his lifetime endeavor disseminated to become the Islam of Muhammad.

SEVEN

The Bishop Marries
the Prophet

O Khadija, most distinguished
among all Quraish women
You attained fame and fortune
surpassing grueling men
Your fate is different though:
above wealth and profit,
The one who husbands you is
this nation's Prophet!

Bishop Waraka, from a poem to Khadija

What Abu Bakr Alsiddiq predicted earlier in the Consultative House came very true. Abu Bakr, the devout Nazarene who was close to Waraka and among the regular worshippers in his Hira' Cave took the task of preparing Muhammad socially and above all, rhetorically. Alsiddiq (the truthful) was Abu Bakr's nickname bestowed by Muhammad later to further solidify his right to succession. Waraka at that time was in his seventies still of robust built but started losing eyesight. Yet he remained the spiritual guide to the Prophet educating him in all theological aspects of the faith. Abu Bakr assumed his brushing up individually and socially in preparation for the imminent mission. The excellent administrator was to be declared the first Caliph the day the Prophet died although Ali was closer to him and as his Shia clan maintain, worthier than Abu Bakr. In fact Ali was a fearless fighter and a prince of eloquence but a womanizer with limited political vision.

Poverty does not produce clear minds to ponder over the many intricate phases of theology and sociology. Following strong recommendations by Waraka and repetitive poverty grumblings and intensive appeals by his uncle Abu Taleb, Muhammad entered the service of wealthy Khadija. He accumulated a vast experience assisting his uncle on many Damascus caravans. He went on handling her commerce with zest and honesty. She was rewarding him with a double pay for a similar task. His integrity in safeguarding her interests was well known among his mates in the caravans. He soon was called: Muhammad Al-Amin "the Faithful"; a surname that was affixed to him forever.

Waraka took the task of convincing Khadija, now 44, twice widowed and mother of several children to marry Muhammad now 25. She hesitated to wed a boy the age of her children but Waraka had the upper hand; she was attached to the Bishop with bonds of reverence and respect. She would listen to him on all aspects of her life as historians repeatedly mentioned: ". . . and that was by instructions from Waraka" (Sira Halabia-history). She accepted and sent Muhammad her maid Nafisa to negotiate his marrying her.

It is appropriate to mention here that Arabian women before Islam used to propose to men and ask their hands in marriage the way men do today. They were even more assertive than most men of our time in saying: 'I have wed you my self'. Many such proposals were cast by women on worthy men including the Muhammad himself during his Medina years.

Nafisa later told the story as it happened: 'she sent me clandestinely to Muhammad on his return in her caravan from Damascus; I told him: Muhammad, what prevents you from marriage? He said: I don't have what to marry with. I said: what if you skip that and receive an invitation to wealth, beauty, nobility and distinction? would you respond? He said: who is she? I said: Khadija. He said: and would I get to that? I said: yes. Let me handle it. And I went to Khadija and informed her; she sent asking him to come at a certain hour' (Ibn Saad—historian).

'At the stated hour Khadija summoned her uncles and Muhammad summoned his; they all showed up and convened among few dignitaries from Quraish. Abu Taleb had the first word: ". . . and Muhammad is a young man unequalled in all

Quraish when it comes to honor, nobility and reason. If money lacks him, money is a passing shadow and a replaceable commodity. He has a desire in Khadija and she has the same in him". Then Bishop Waraka solemnly announced: "Thanks to God who set us as you stated and distinguished us above all. We are the masters and leaders of the Arabs and you all share this eminence. So, people of Quraish, witness that I have wed today Khadija Bint Khowailed to Muhammad Bin Abdullah". Abu Taleb was noticeably elated and said: "Thanks to God who dismissed our sorrows and dispelled our grievances"?! He then remarked: "he (Muhammad), by God, will have after this (marriage) a distinguished status and a great magnitude". (Ibn Hisham).

This wedding had many important aspects: It was a purely Nazarene ceremony presided by a Nazarene Bishop who 'tied by the name of God,—according to the Ebionite' belief—what no human may untie'. This confirms the religion of the newlyweds. No wonder it lasted until one of the two (Khadija) died. It was a Nazarene marriage par excellence with mutual consent between the bride and the groom solemnized by a bishop and witnessed by a distinguished gathering of Quraish.

What clerics and historians ignored is that Waraka who was on a relentless lookout for a disciple to herald his lifelong labor and who saw in Muhammad after due investigation an accomplished candidate, opted to rid the young man from poverty and hard work and steer him closely within his spiritual domain of learning and contemplation. It was initially the wish of Waraka not Khadija to conclude this marriage despite the adamant refusal of her snooty father who said dismissingly: "Me, marrying the orphan of Abu Taleb?

Not on my dead body!" But Khadija acquiesced to her uncle's wish and told her father: "refrain from that or the shame of Quraish would fall upon your head". (Ibn Hisham).

Muhammad moved from his modest foster home to Khadija's lavish mansion in 'the high society quarter' to live in 'the high above' apartments and sleep on an 'elevated bed with stuffed and puffy mattresses.' This move mellowed somehow his disillusionment but did not dissipate his alienation. Clerics embellished and overstated the compatibility of this wedding. The fact was different: a typical marriage of convenience orchestrated by a Bishop who charted a master plan to execute his ultimate ambition: inject in the Arabian society a modified Christian religion that he already had on scrolls; an Ebionite Nazarene belief thorough and readily befitting the Bedouin lifestyle. Its simplicity was unprecedented: a Bedouin had only to testify: "there is no God but Allah and Muhammad is his Messenger" and he would enter the faith the way he enters the tent of his chieftain. The old wise man needed a young bright colleague ready to learn and comprehend; a diligent and trustworthy kinship with the stated goal to succeed him as the Ebionite Bishop of Mecca. Muhammad qualified for all requisites.

It is unacceptable by any norms that a marriage between a young man and a widow of 44 be termed compatible. The intense virility of Muhammad who later married twelve women could not be satiated with a female the age of his mother. To say the least Muhammad was sexually miserable in this marriage: the young, bright maidens of Mecca were all around him haunting his imagination including one that was dearest to his heart: Zainab bint Jahsh.

Yet Waraka persuaded both the destitute young man and his wealthy old boss to join in matrimony. The Prophet fell within the Bishop's grips and was convinced he was at the threshold of an open-ended future full of hopes and aspirations. The Cave of Hira' was the perfect place for both men to ponder the future, forsake people, memorize and comprehend Waraka's Arabic version of the Gospel and 'reflect on God one full month each year.'(Ibn Hisham).

Reclusion and solitary life were suitable to Muhammad who spent most of his youth a disgruntled loner. He found in Hira' his rediscovered salute and in the Bishop's company a revived paternal love he always missed. This is where his spiritual capabilities were unleashed and his theological edification extended. Hira' was a replication of the old Ebionite abstinence at the Qumran convent. Yet the strenuous and austere spiritual regimen Muhammad was subjected to in Waraka's company renewed his early convulsions. The intense meditation strain would cause waves of spasms and shudders in his entire body. "He would perspire even in cold nights and ask his wife to wrap him with thick garments. Khadija would jump to her uncle seeking help. He would comfort and reassure her." (Ibn Hisham). The convulsions would not die away: they rather increased after he moved to Medina and were attributed to revelation descents. He would again shout at the approach of each: "cover me . . . cover me . . ." his new wives would rush to wrap him with heavy garments.

EIGHT

The Education of
Muhammad

"You have been given the mastery of words."
Koran addressing Muhammad

For over 20 years Muhammad was devoted to the Bishop's coaching and tutoring all the while heartened and monitored by Abu Bakr. This is the most important part in Muhammad's life where his spiritual culture and religious vocation blossomed. It looked as if Muhammad, like John and Jesus, had his share of a similar "20 lost years"

65

unapproachable by clerics and historians and spent in a cave very similar to Qumran. It is no wonder that the 'the Gospel according to Hebrews' that Waraka was rewriting in his poetic language was pondered, read and later memorized by the Prophet. It is also no wonder for lack of any contradicting theory, that it was the 'Master Book', originator of the Arabic Koran that repeatedly supports its veracity: (Koran 12/36 & 11/17 & 12/46).

Scholars insisted on Muhammad's illiteracy to hold up absolute conviction of the divine revelation upon him and maintain that the Koran is all but the work of God transferred through the medium Gabriel. God has always propagated his Word through worldly mediums since Moses who would communicate with him through spells. Here He used for Muhammad a 'skillful erudite' who 'taught him what he did not know'.

Therefore we should draw a line between what Muhammad knew and what he ignored and learned later. Reading and writing skills were certainly bestowed upon him by Abu Taleb as he did upon his son Ali. It is not rational to suppose that Abu Taleb who raised both children in his household and gave Muhammad 'more attention' than his own son Ali would groom one into an eloquence writer and deprive the other from basic learning. Muhammad undoubtedly had read Ali's book: 'Nahj-ul-Balagha' or 'The Exemplar of Eloquence', the first Arabic book ever written next to the Koran and personally described its superior style as "under the Creator's words and above the creature's". This is a weighty testimony by an educated Prophet proclaimed in the Koran itself as 'Given the mastery of words'. On the other hand how could a really illiterate man run the important commerce of Khadija and handle the intricate dealings with the shrewd and highly educated Damascene merchants?

This scholastic muddling could have been knowingly or inadvertently a misinterpretation of the Arabic word 'Ummi' and Muhammad's portrayal as 'the Ummi Prophet'. While it plainly means 'illiterate' in our times its 6th century use was to characterize those who did not have a 'Book', 'Uminim' in Hebrew. Thus the Jews and Christians who had revealed books, or 'Kitab', were 'Kitabis' or literate. Pagan Arabs including Nazarenes who had not were 'Ummis' although they were readers and writers. There is no better reference to confirm this than the Koran itself: (Koran 7/157 & 3/20 etc . . .). It states: 'And He (God) assigned among Ummis (non-Kitab Arabs) a messenger, *reading* His verses upon them . . .' (Koran 21:62/2). The book has been written in Arabic so Muhammad could *read* and comprehend *alone* and without anybody's help, "*Read* your book, sufficient is your soul today to account on you." (Koran 17:14).

Trusted historian Ibn Abbas gave further clarifications: 'Ummis (Arabs) did not believe God sent a messenger nor revealed a Book, so they *wrote* one (for need to claim they were not Ummis) with *their own hands*' (Al-Tabari, historian). Furthermore, Muhammad proclaimed the first revealed verses that say: "*Read—Ikra'a*—by the name of your God who created . . . *Read,* and your God is the generous; He taught man what he did not know". (Koran 1/69). Should Muhammad be a non-reader as tenacious historians reported him to answer: 'I am no reader', the medium would certainly know and wouldn't otherwise ask him to do so. Yet he did read! Whatever the many derivatives of the verb 'Kara'a', in over sixty Koranic verses Muhammad was asked to *read* and explain. Scholars, here again, insist that *Kara'a* could also mean 'recite' not necessarily from a written document but from memory. This is a fact and Muhammad was reciting most of the times although it is dispelled by the verse: ' . . . and a Koran We have detailed that you *read* to the people unhurriedly (so they could grasp)'. (Koran 17/106).

As to the other education in divinity and revelation Muhammad studied (*darasa*) this knowledge with the Bishop slowly but steadily throughout the second 20 years of his life. It is also irrational to suppose that Waraka picked a non-reader student to read and memorize a multitude of sophisticated written texts at a time he started losing his eyesight. The verb 'darasa', "meant only: <u>studying theology and holy books from written texts</u>." (Le Coran—D. Masson 6/105, French historian). The Koran further asserts that: "How could you judge? Do you have a book (another special revealed book) in which you (darasa) study—?" (Koran 68/35). The prophet defended his knowledge, confirming that he studied on those "who read the Book earlier." (Koran 10/94). He also did not deny that his total knowledge was *acquisitioned* as he had no grasp of the unknown: "I don't tell you I have the closets of God, nor do I know the concealed." (Koran, 6/50).

When Muhammad's followers doubted the authenticity of his doctrine he would refer them to the 'People of the Book': "Consult the people of the scripture if you don't know". (Koran 16/43.) And when Muslims diverged in explicating his revelation he would refer them to the only Gospel—according to Hebrews—he new: "let the people of the Gospel judge what God *revealed in it* (the Koran)". (Koran, 5/47).

The Bishop/leader of Ummi Nazarenes was not only a close kin to Muhammad but unquestionably the guide and tutor. His role and mission in the revelation of theology were best validated by Aisha the young daughter of Abu Bakr; wife of the Prophet and most trusted keeper of his 'Hadith'. She said in Medina: ' . . . and soon Waraka died and the revelation faded away."

The real lacking of Muhammad is that he was not a poet at a time where the poetic Koran language was imparted for him to read and memorize. In fact he hated and despised poets although he had to have a famous one at his side, Hassan bin Thabet, whose task was to praise the Prophet, blast his enemies and support his mission. This however did not dissuade Muhammad from voicing his opinion: "Poets are misleaders followed by the misled; don't you see them rambling in every valley (of thought), saying what they don't do?" Nevertheless both Waraka and Abu Bakr wanted to make sure Muhammad attains a high degree in eloquence. They would send him back many times to Bani Saad Bedouin encampment where he was once breast fed by Halima to learn and excel in "Jazala" or concise expressiveness from its pure origins and possess "the mastery of words".

Concise expressiveness; the ability to inject maximum meaning through minimum words was the highly coveted feature of any public figure at the time. The impatient Arab mind loathes details and adores succinct approaches. When Amr bin Al-As, conqueror of Egypt, prepared his campaign he sent a secret agent who spent six months studying the country from Alexandria to Aswan. His report to Amr was made of *one* rhythmic line: "peoples whose land is gold, whose women are dolls and who are slaves to the victor." Amr immediately ordered the march. To his governor of Basra, Iraq, the Caliph Omar sent a similar one-line rhythmic letter: "your enemies increased, your supporters decreased, either moderate or abdicate". It was a known fact that the tragic failure of the fourth Caliph Othman in his public addresses was the main factor in the waning of his Caliphate. The Koran recommends to Muslims to run their affairs through consultations in only three words: "(and their) *matter* (is) *consultation* (among) *them*." Even today in the Arabian Peninsula a word or two can be the answer for a long query. A friend told me he was sitting once in the office of the traffic police chief when a car accident was mentioned. He sent an officer out to investigate and report. The officer came back ten minutes later, saluted and gave his one-word report: "sadm" or collision!

As soon as Waraka ascertained that Muhammad was up to the mission and that his personal and spiritual edification developed to his satisfaction, he started trickling various announcements. Many other contributors entered the campaign: Khadija the high ranked emissary between Muhammad and the Bishop and between them and her counterparts in the commerce nobility, her father who later acquiesced to her wedding, Abu Taleb who foresaw to his nephew "a distinguished status and a great magnitude" and last but not least Abu Bakr the impeccable planner. "Other contributors to the cause were: Vicar Bahira who read his mole, Vicar Addas Ninawi who once healed Muhammad from early conjunctivitis and Salman Al Farisi, a Persian Nazarene and a follower of the Bishop." (Sira Makiah-History).

Perhaps the first announcement was proclaimed by the Bishop himself as recorded by historian Ibn Hisham: "Maysara, the faithful servant of Khadija, informed her on his return with Muhammad from Damascus of the wondrous foretelling of Bahira. She immediately carried his story to the Bishop who stood and said in full confidence: 'If that was true, Khadija, Muhammad is the Messenger of this nation. I had always envisioned (?) this nation was bound to have a messenger whose time has come" (Ibn Hisham-historian & Sira Halabia-History). Waraka was so stirred by the event that he composed the following poem addressed to Khadija:

"I reminisce of a concern that is deeply persistent.
A Khadija storyline, long obsessing an expectant
That would stir both flanks of the Mecca dwelling
The story you recounted of a Bishop's saying . . .
A monk* whose testimony I honor and never doubt
That Muhammad will hold sway, defeat and rout
All his antagonists, any rival or contender;
His light will glow bright over this land and yonder
Whoever opposes him would be a clear-cut loser.
If I witness this tribulation I would be first to engage
Even if Quraish rises up and fills Mecca with rage.
I refer to the Supreme those who will oppose and foment
Those unbelievers in Him who set out the firmament
If they persist while am alive, I will wedge them my fight
But if I pass away**, such is every mortal's plight!

* Bahira **of old age

The translation may not give this poem its original thrust and beauty or the rationales behind it. It clearly shows Waraka's concerns about the Message as being his own and the Messenger as part of him that he is ready to defend if he could.

The second announcement came when Muhammad hit his forties: Gabriel intimated to him while contemplating at 'Hira Cave': "hail Muhammad I am Gabriel and you are the Messenger of God to this nation". Petrified, he ran back home and told his story to Khadija who told him in full poise: "rejoice my cousin and stand fast; by the One who holds my soul I do hope you will be the prophet of this nation". Then she rushed to her uncle and informed him. He did not hesitate to tell her: "behold, behold, by the One who holds Waraka's soul in His hand if what you just said is true the Great Tribulation that confronted Moses has come and he is by God the messenger of this nation. Ask him to stand fast." (Ibn Hisham, Ibn Saad, Tobari & Ibn Athir-historians).

The third proclamation happened in the Mecca shrine when Muhammad descended from the cave by the end of Ramadan, his month of worshipping and fasting and was performing the seven-stride ritual around the Qaaba. The Bishop who happened to be striding also stopped and prompted him: "tell me my nephew of what you saw and heard". Muhammad recounted to him. The Bishop was elated and declared: "by the One who holds my soul you are the Prophet of this nation; you have been given the Great Tribulation that was given Moses. You would negate it, hurt it, oust it and fight it. Should I witness that day I would uphold Allah towards His victory". Waraka then held Muhammad's head and kissed it. Muhammad went home appeased." (Ibn Hisham & Tobari-historians).

The fourth announcement came when Muhammad, accompanied by his friend Abu Bakr, headed to Waraka for consultations on his many strange spasms like shuddering, fainting, and swooning. "I would hear a call behind me: Muhammad . . . Muhammad . . . and would run away into the open . . ." Waraka would comfort, appease and counsel him: "do not run. If you are called, hang about, listen to what it says then *report to me*" (Halabia-history). Abu Bakr disseminated those important signals to his close friends in the Consultative House.

The fifth proclamation took place when Muhammad set out to recite the new Koran verses among a Mecca crowd. The usual spasm seized him and he started trembling anew. He ran back home shaking and asked his wife to cover him heavily. She comforted him as usual and took him to Waraka who further pacified him repeating: "this, dear nephew, is the Tribulation of Moses. I wish I was younger to attend to the divine tidings". Then he addressed Khadija: "certainly, any man assuming this task (revolting against the rich, enforcing an unconventional doctrine among tribes etc . . .); should face enmity." (Tabari-historian).

The sixth and most important public statement was witnessed and made known by Ali son of Abu Taleb, the Prophet's nephew and youth companion. Ali, the first Muslim convert, recorded: "when Muhammad heard the call 'Say I bear witness that there is no God but Allah and Muhammad is his Messenger', Muhammad answered: 'with obedience'. When he heard: 'say praise be to God the cherisher and sustainer of the worlds, most gracious, most merciful, master of the Day of Judgment'; he was troubled. He rushed to see the Bishop and recounted what he heard. Waraka was elated and said: "behold then behold! I hereby bear witness that you are the one prophesized by the Son of Mary (?) and you are on the path of Moses and you are a sent Messenger ordered to *Jihad* as of this day and if I am given to witness that I will wage it with you" (Sira Halabia & Tabari—history). The word "Jihad", meaning "engage in imposing the Word of Allah", was pronounced by Waraka for the first time; yet it entered the annals of Islam and remains to this day in its various meanings the plight and religious endeavor of every Muslim.

This statement was released by the Bishop shortly before Muhammad went on his all-out Jihad. It was the official public release on the Mission and the Message carried out by a qualified and dedicated Messenger. A *statement witnessed and propagated by no less qualified* followers than experienced Abu Bakr and young Ali. At that time, Waraka was approaching his 98, deaf, blind and disabled. Yet his call for Jihad served to inflame all participants to do their shares and remind Muhammad that he was not alone in the upcoming struggle against the spoiled infidels of Quraish. In fact he remained until his death guiding and monitoring him through the early phases of the assignment. Bishop Waraka died happy and satisfied: his disciple took over the mission with flying colors.

The most precious advice the disciple received from his professor was patience. Waraka embodied this quality giving his cherished task his total lifespan. Muhammad learned 'not to rush things: along the way to success one should be armed with a substantial measure of patience'. A valuable advice given repeatedly in the Koran: "Persevere as did apostles of inflexible purpose; and be in no haste about the unbelievers . . ." (Koran 46/35).

NINE

The Outbreak

"Arabs' way of thinking is such that they don't accept governance or undergo a leadership that is not backed by a religious foundation."
Ibn Khaldoon, historian/philosopher

T hus it happened. It wouldn't have without a meticulous planning and confluence of all positive components: historic cycle of events, the Koran's testimonials and as in all preceding religions, the human mediums employed. They all confirmed that Muhammad sustained a beatific thrust by the caring and capable hands of Waraka, Khadija, Abu Taleb, Abu Bakr and others.

Yet 617A.D. was the "Year of Sorrow" during which Muhammad, 47, lost his wife, his uncle and his professor. His remaining close supporters were: uncle Hamza the intrepid "lion hunter", nephew Ali the young warrior and last but not least Abu Bakr the astute schemer.

Up until that year Muhammad was not proclaimed— neither did he claim to be—a prophet. The Koran of Mecca referred to him as "Messenger", "Announcer" and "Admonisher". In fact the real intention of the Bishop was to assert his disciple as his successor and overall chief of the Arab Nazarenes, to bring about his guidelines, disseminate the new Book unto them and promulgate the updated and simplified Ebionite Christianity in plain Arabic language. The plan was to unify the dispersed Nazarenes and Jews by bringing together their various dogmas into an all-encompassing and simplified belief. Muhammad recognized clearly his mission: he went on announcing, preaching and educating people, showing them the "Straight Way" and opening their minds to the "Worthy Religion"; motivating them to do good deeds and reciting stories of the elders and ancient prophets.

He knew quite well his task consisted in reminding people of the Torah and Gospel principles. He was constantly goaded in the Koran to forewarn people: "therefore do give admonition, you are one to admonish". (Koran 88/21). And: "remind, as reminiscing benefits the believers". (Koran 51/55). Slowly but surely his eloquent message went through, supported by the high prominence of Khadija, her immense fortune and the careful promotion of Abu Bakr at the elite

Consultative House. The message was well acclaimed by the have-nots and few of Quraish's Nazarenes. Najashi, king of Abyssinia, opened his country to those early followers prosecuted by Mecca's moguls. Shortly after the Bishop's death Muhammad became the supreme leader of all monolithic, devoted and submissive Nazarenes (Muslimeen) as recorded in the Book: "And I am commanded to be the first of the Muslimeen (the submissive)". (Koran 29/12).

On the other hand the Year of Sorrow brought Muhammad lots of solace, freedom and élan. During the first seven years of spreading the Message he suffered the constant bullying of old, deaf and blind Waraka "listen to what it says then *report to me!*" He also endured the motherly keen eye of Khadija who gave him his only child: daughter Fatima and whose financial support was worse on him than flagellation. Her motherly love engendered a dissatisfied and incompatible sex relationship where his raging eroticism was constantly subdued. Only Abu Taleb, the poor foster father who guided him through his staggering youth was his heart-felt loss.

That same year carried also a change of mind and course carefully crafted and insinuated by Abu Bakr. Quraish and its satellite tribes did not simply need a belief to follow but also a governance scheme to abide by and rally around. The Bedouin did not embrace Islam as a religion but as a new power enabling him to revolt against hunger, loneliness and tough life. A power that made him yearns towards the silk garments and the sweet living of the Romans and the Persians. Thus the Announcer and Admonisher titles advocated by Waraka have been gradually phased out to the Messenger of Allah and ultimately the Prophet. These governance characteristics were very much in line with the Koran encompassing among the basic sets of belief lots of personal and social guidelines a Muslim should abide by. Muhammad took his friend's proposal cautiously and reluctantly at the outset. Abu Bakr assured him that soon enough many of the Consultative House tycoons will second his motion and under any circumstances he will remain his close supporter. Perseverance and resolve remain the basic ingredients.

Muhammad went on with renewed determination. Soon enough however, ridiculing, hostilities, even physical attacks started showering over his head. At one time at the Taif vineyards town he was denied a grape to eat and was ousted by hordes of stoning children. Back in Mecca he avoided walking the streets let alone sermonizing. Most of his followers have either fled to Abyssinia or stayed put inside their homes.

Quraish's chieftains and hardliners especially those who begrudged the Hashemite house of Muhammad set out one day after sunset at the Qaaba and summoned him to negotiate: "If you came up with this parley to seek money, we can participate each on his own until you are the richest among us. If it is a position you want we will appoint you as our chief. If you seek a kingdom we will elect you our king. And should this Jinni (gnome) assails you we would invest our money to heal you of it or be excused." (Ibn Hisham-historian).

Muhammad was not taken aback. He expected such hoodwinked proposal and prepared his early answer with Abu Bakr. He looked them in the eyes and said: "I did not come up with this issue to seek money, honor or sovereignty. Allah sent me to be your admonisher. I relayed the message of my

God and warned you. Should you heed it, it would be your fortune in this world and the hereafter. Should you revoke, I would assent to God's ruling between you and me." (Ibn Hisham-historian). This encounter gave Muhammad the first real taste of confrontational leadership. Nowadays it is not himself alone; it is Allah and His Prophet: a strong coalition that would shake the spine of the mightiest of men.

From that day on Muhammad followed the new course charted by Abu Bakr. A total departure from the mission Waraka spent his prime years preparing him for. The Bishop went down to total oblivion. He was no longer mentioned in any of Islam's literature. He was persona non grata: the man who never was. Scholars shrunk the distance and swallowed the documents to please Caliphs and princes, appease people and safeguard the sanctity of the revelation.

Throughout history, when two cultures clash, the loser is obliterated and the winner writes the books that glorify his own cause and disparage the conquered foe. History thus becomes 'a fable agreed upon' as Napoleon said. In the case of Waraka history became a one-sided account; his home was demolished, his books were burnt and no reference to him was ever mentioned throughout the next 100 years after his demise except to the meaningful slip of tongue by Aisha: "As soon as Waraka died the revelation faded away".

Muhammad was preoccupied in securing new patterns of revelations that complement the Mecca Koran. Revelations ceased for a long time (some say two years); some of Muhammad's friends may have said to him "It seems that your Allah has forsaken you." The Prophet passed through a terrible spiritual crisis. His biographers said: "During that time

81

Muhammad thought to commit suicide by throwing himself from the top of Mount Hira or Mount Abi-Qubees, because he felt desperate and lonely" (Prophecy and Prophets, page 177). Ali has now come of age and accomplished the mastery of both sword and word. But Waraka was irreplaceable when it comes to Torah and Gospel interpretations.

When he moved with Abu Bakr to Medina, fresh revelations were still in short supply. To fill the gap, 'he assigned young Zaid bin Thabet, brother of his personal poet, who knew Hebrew thanks to his excellent business relations with the Jews of Medina, to learn Aramaic as well and provide the required facts and references.' (Masoudi-historian). Ali, and later Othman and probably Muawia would verbalize the inspirations into Koranic texts. With such basic preparations Allah swore to Muhammad "by the glorious morning light and by the night that He had not forsaken you nor was He displeased with you." (Koran).

Also from that day Islam started its deviation from a religion of the meek and deprived into one led and directed by the magnates of the Consultative House. The Prophet himself who earlier advocated equality among Muslim regardless of status or creed resorted later to reclassify followers: "people are metals, he said, their crème in Jahiliya (pre-Islam era of paganism) is their crème in Islam once converted." (Masoudi-historian). This meant that Abu Bakr, Othman and Omar, the leaders of the Consultative House and the moguls of Mecca before Islam are unquestionably the would-be leaders of Islam. The Ebionite Nazarene spirit that originally characterized the new faith has sadly given way to the wealthy tycoons' aggressive domination.

Many Muslims today refuse to accept this tactic as premeditated. "Allah has ways and means in His people", they retort. The Muslim mind dominated by postulates may not dare say it was all Abu Bakr's planning and implementation supported by Othman as well as Omar who later declared: "If it wasn't to Islam, Tagleb would have eaten the people".

TEN

The Founding Fathers

*"Men are like metals. Their best in Jahiliya are
their best in Islam once converted."*

Muhammad

Abu Bakr Al Siddiq saw the fruits of his steady
efforts ripen. He had carefully steered the fledgling
Islamic ship through a maze of clandestine meetings,
quid-pro-quo deals and intense jealousies. Muhammad is
doing such a fine job that exceeded all his expectations. The
Prophet is following his best friend's new scheme with zest and
equanimity knowing full well where he was steering him into.

Abu Bakr did not hesitate to communicate these successes to the Consultative House stratocracy outlining all upcoming benefits to Quraish in establishing a theocratic system that would be the nucleus for a growing empire promoting Islam through Fath (conquest) and Jihad in the name of Allah and His Prophet.

Who was Abu Bakr?

"No one has been a better companion to me than Abu Bakr" said Muhammad, bestowing a great reward enabling his friend to earn the succession to power after him. Abu Bakr had a controversial personality, charismatic and enigmatic at a time. He was compassionate where clemency is due and ruthless when callousness is the cup of coffee. But in all situations he would maintain a perceptive plotter approach.

He was two years younger than Muhammad, a practicing Ebionite and a staunch Waraka follower since his youth. He came from a noble family and was sincere and truthful. He developed an impeccable reputation in Mecca's financial circles and a name for honesty in his dealings with people to the point that they kept their money with him as in a bank today. He won high respect and became a rich merchant. He was attached to Muhammad since boyhood with a friendship that proved to be lifelong and history-making.

Abu Bakr was only second to young Ali in embracing Islam. He supported the mission and accepted the Bishop's plans but visualized for Muhammad and Islam a larger scheme than Waraka's. He began to preach Islam to his many friends and high ranked collaborators. Among them Othman bin Affan the wealthy and future third Caliph, Talha, Abdul Rahman bin Auf and Saad bin Waqqas the conqueror of Iraq and Persia. These Consultative House men became later the "Pillars of Islam" and the first "paradise nominees".

Muhammad was passing by the Qaaba one day where Abu Jahl, a notorious pagan chief in Mecca suddenly rushed to him and tried to strangle him with a piece of cloth. Abu Bakr saw this from a distance. He overwhelmed Abu Jahl and snatched the cloth from his friend's neck. Abu Jahl's men took hold of Abu Bakr and beat him severely until he fell down senseless. A crowd interfered and stopped the assailants. Abu Bakr new full well that if any harm came to Muhammad the fruits of long years of preparation would go astray.

Following this and many similar incidents Abu Bakr resorted to a bold scheme: he used his immense fortune to buy prosecuted slaves from their non-Muslim masters and free them to join and reinforce Islam. A case in point was Bilal the Abyssinian who was tortured daily by his master Umayya. Abu Bakr bought Bilal at a heavy price and set him free. Bilal, with his high pitched voice became later in Medina the first "Muazzin" (caller to prayer) at the Prophet's mosque.

In the process Abu Bakr brought upon himself the special anger and hatred of other Meccan chiefs. His life was so unbearable in town that he decided to join the emigrants in Abyssinia. On the way out he was intercepted by chief Daghna who told him: "a man like you should not be cast out; you help the poor and support those in trouble. I will take you back to Mecca under my protection. Daghna declared this to all Mecca chiefs who agreed to let Abu Bakr alone if he does not preach his faith publicly. He did not act on this condition for long.

In the tenth year of his mission Muhammad received Gabriel one night; the angel mounted him on a winged mule

(Al-Buraq) and set him out to Jerusalem thence to the highest heaven to see Allah and the earlier prophets and then back to Mecca before dawn. This event named Israa (night travel) & Miraj (side trip) was communicated to people by Muhammad the morning of his landing. The unconventional incident raised many eyebrows and drew jeers among his enemies: "look" they howled out, 'what nonsense he talks; who is going to believe in such a midsummer dream?" They went to his supporter Abu Bakr: "would you really believe this talk?" "I would believe anything the Messenger says," he replied and further reconfirmed his nickname "Alsiddiq" (the truthful).

The Meccans' pressure to put out the mission intensified. In the burning heat of a midday sun there was a knock on Abu Bakr's door. It was Muhammad who advised him his acquiescence to leave to Medina. "I am going with you" said Abu Bakr. "Of course," was the reply, "set about getting things ready". This migration known in Islam as the *hijra* is considered to mark the birth of an independent Islamic community and 622B.C. was thus the first year of the Islamic calendar.

Among all reluctant companions Abu Bakr supported Muhammad during the most critical days of his life. Throughout the thorny years of armed Jihad in Medina he was always close to him, counseling, comforting . . . and monitoring. His impeccable strategies and sharp mind helped Muhammad in countless situations. Perhaps the smartest stunt he had ever attempted was when the Prophet died without naming a successor: he called all believers to prayer and for the first time replaced Muhammad on the pulpit and prompted everybody: "he who worshipped Muhammad,

Muhammad is now dead; but he who worshipped Allah, Allah is alive and immortal". At this stance he asked for 'Biaa' or pledge of allegiance for Caliph and got it unanimously while Ali the first contender, Muhammad's nephew and son-in-law was away preparing the Prophet's burial. This stunt succeeded with the consent and support of the strongest man in Islam: Omar ibn Al-Khattab, aborting a potential power struggle. Abu Bakr lived only two years as a Caliph. He spent most of this time waging the "Apostasy War", fighting back to Islam all the renegades who deserted upon the death of Muhammad, chief among them Tagleb. As he lay dying he declared Omar his successor in a crafty, businesslike ritual that was distinctive of him all his life.

The death of Abu Bakr culminated years of meticulous planning, careful studies, secret encounters and aggressive confrontations; a job extremely well done. The first Caliph in Islam and real founding father died peacefully having brought back all defectors, conquered Iraq and half of Persia and above all secured a capable successor to carry the torch.

Omar ibn al-Khattab is likened in fighting early Muslims than embracing and spreading Islam by the sword, to Apostle Paul's persecuting Christians, miraculous joining then spreading Christianity by the sermon. They both share similar boldness and resolve.

Omar begun his life as a Quraish ambassador to various tribes in the Peninsula and is said to have great belief in tribal solidarity. His reputation expounded over two very strong characteristics: physical might and oratory confidence. He was a heavy weight wrestler competing in matches as a hobby and winning almost all of them. Omar possessed also a concise, rhythmic speech although he never fully mastered the language as Ali did. He sometimes used to ask his assistants to explain some of the Koran's verses. Before his conversion Omar is reported as having 4 to 5 wives some of whom were divorced for fresh ones. In all he had 9 sons and 4 daughters one of them the unattractive Hafsa, a widowed that nobody agreed to marry despite his pleas to friends . . . only Muhammad accepted.

Omar, the cocksure with a nose for the big deal was a personal friend of Abu Bakr and member of the House. To confirm this special relationship he later said of him: "Abu Bakr is our master and the emancipator of our master". In real fact Omar became later the emancipator of both men after he found in Islam what would become his own identity. He was 27 and already a very wealthy man when Muhammad unleashed his undertaking. He remained a bitter opponent to the mission despite Abu Bakr's implications and was even assigned by the moguls with the duty of assassinating Muhammad. He was brainwashed that Muhammad is splitting the people who so far lived in harmony; now because of him a son is torn from father and brother from brother, his followers are running away to other lands and he is the cause of all troubles.

Abu Bakr however managed to persuade him to hold his horses and convinced him that this mission was heading to an empire where he (Omar) should play a major role soon. Abu Bakr praised his theory of tribal association as a reason plus; he persuaded him the only way to unify the tribes is Muhammad's way. In fact historians perceived a coalition between the two men especially regarding the charted, neat and utterly secretive package of power succession after Muhammad . . . But Omar resisted Abu Bakr's overtures as two hurdles were still ahead: one/ how to come out of his pledge before the magnates of Quraish to take Muhammad's life and, two/ Islam is an institution with a wide entrance but no exit at all. The big man wanted time to ponder his options before he becomes connected to the nascent movement . . .

Abu Bakr insinuated to Muhammad to lay out a supplication to further attract the most feared and respected man in Quraish. The crafty planner anticipated the succession scuffle and wanted Omar to his side. The Prophet disseminated his plea: "Oh Allah, fortify Islam with Omar". Omar took delivery of it in no time and started looking for a face saving approach.

Clerics set out the following story: 'Omar put on his sword and headed to kill the Prophet. On the way he met a friend who *knew what he had in mind*. He told him: "you better take care of your kin first; your sister and her husband have gone over to Islam". Omar changed direction to his sister's house and heard recitation. He forced the door open and asked: "what was it that you were reciting?" His sister Fatima uttered in fear: "nothing". He shouted in rage: "I have heard it alright; you both have accepted Muhammad's faith . . ." He then began to beat his brother-in-law, Saeed. Fatima ran to his rescue and got a blow on her head. When Omar saw her blood he was moved and restrained. He said calmly: "let me have a look at the Koran". She handed it to him and he read some verses then said: "Surely these are divine words". He got up and headed to Muhammad who was sitting in the company of some men among them his uncle Hamza the lion hunter who said: 'if he comes armed, I shall slay him with his own sword'. Muhammad saw Omar and shouted from a distance: "Omar, what brings you here?" "O Prophet of Allah" he replied, "I have come to embrace Islam". The joy of Muhammad and his followers was so great the loud shouts of "Allah-o-Akbar" filled the air over Mecca.

As time passed, Omar's many supporters accused him with cultivating an atmosphere of intimidation among the Prophet's entourage. In fact the relationship between Muhammad and Omar was superficially sweet but deeply sour. Arrogant Omar started working his way into the Medina power scene. His larger-than-life, imposing, challenging and fearless personality was the exact opposite of Muhammad's traits. Omar was a difficult man to get along with; a man with casual disregard of those with whom he deals including Muhammad. He displayed this same disregard upon the Prophet even on his deathbed. Muhammad was always dreading and avoiding confrontations with Omar to the point of shunning; and if it wasn't to the "gentlemen's agreement" between Abu Bakr and Omar vis-à-vis the future succession the latter would have easily consolidated all powers even ahead of Muhammad's demise.

That 'Agreement' between the two Consultative House tycoons was much deeper than Muhammad thought. The Prophet sensed in his last couple of years discernible disingenuous behavior by his old friend and tutor Abu Bakr using his daughter Aisha to scout Ali and his wife Fatima, daughter of the Prophet, ridicule them and keep them distanced from Muhammad. It is said that the mysterious death of the Prophet's only son and heir Ibrahim from curly

Egyptian Maria on his second birthday was plotted by Aisha. The coalition headed by Omar of Abu Bakr, Aisha and Hafsa (both Muhammad's wives), went on rock-solid and inseparable till the death of the Prophet.

Historians agree it was Omar who spread Islam to as far as Persia, Egypt and Anatolia and defeated towering empires such as the Sassanids (Persians) and the Byzantines in a rapid expansion that startled the old world. His influence remains to be seen everywhere in the Middle East today. Most Arab and Muslim countries owe their existence to the expansion made during his Caliphate. Omar was not only a warrior but an administrative genius as well. He established the bases of the Islamic judicial system and devised a systematic measurement of time through the lunar calendar which most Muslims still use today. He succeeded in maintaining average unity of the new, dispersed Muslim communities and built a sound economic system which encouraged prosperity. He is said to roam Medina's markets unguarded carrying a whip in his hand where he would lash any seemingly wrongdoer at will; a magnanimous and controversial figure in Islam indeed.

The Persians, who could not confront him in battlegrounds, sent him a trained assassin who stabbed him in 644B.C. while entering the Medina Mosque. On his death bed he named a 6-men counsel and directed them to choose one of them as his successor. The most prominent and wealthy figure was Othman, elected after long and humiliating deliberations among the counsel to become the third Caliph. Before Omar expired, his freedman killer ended up stabbing himself as well; he disclosed the name of his instigator: Persian general Harmuzan.

Othman bin Affan was born six years after the birth of Muhammad. He belonged to the Umayyad branch of Quraish. The Umayyads were thought to be the equals of the Hashemite. The national flag of Quraish was in their keeping.

When Othman grew up he became a cloth merchant. His business flourished and he soon was the top businessman in the city. Syria was his import haven; he amassed wealth and reached a high position. He was the exact opposite of Omar: fussy, but most of the time humble and softhearted and . . . a cherished friend of Abu Bakr.

The Umayyads were in fierce competition with the Hashemite over wealth and position; Othman the Umayyad though was one of the first Muslims and the first to leave to Abyssinia following the repeated hounding by his kinfolk. The Hashemite Prophet loved Othman. He classed him among the elite to earn paradise and gave him Khadija's daughter Roqaya in marriage. He returned to join Muhammad after his migration to Medina and fought with him all the battles except Badr due to his wife's illness. Othman was not a fighter but a major financier of all military expeditions including the all-important Tabuk campaign wherein he contributed one thousand camels.

As a companion of Muhammad, Othman was also a scribe writing whatever revelation the Prophet would come up with. The Koranic text was verified by Omar with the help of Zaid bin Thabet and a final copy was kept with Omar's daughter Hafsa. Othman however took that copy and rewrote it again using many sources as well as his own memory. He inflicted tremendous changes that altered the initial Ebionite Mecca Koran into a different one to mesh with the Medina revelations and the conquests' necessities.

Clearly Othman was not born to lead; hence Omar's reluctance to name him outright. When the choice was at last done Othman rose to make his pitch and address the gathering; all were eager to hear what the new Caliph had to say. But the weight of the new responsibility made his body shake and sweat. All he could utter was: "O people, it is not easy to manage a new horse. There will be occasions to speak to you. I am not very good at speechmaking", a poor show indeed and a shaky jump start among people who consider eloquence a nobler art than knighthood or swordsmanship. Othman's Caliphate gradually withered down and was marred by a terrible uprising that led to his murder. The very gentle and soft-hearted man often overlooked the faults of others. His hand was too weak to take proper and timely actions. Provincial unrests grew engulfing the young and quivering empire. Clever people took advantage of his weakening grip on the state affairs.

One of these brainy individuals was Abdullah bin Saba, a personable Yemeni Jew and a consummate outsider who played a leading role in the drama. He came to Medina and under a show of becoming a good Muslim he studied the situation and saw the Hashemite natural right in the Caliphate and Ali, not Othman as the Caliph. He preached that like Moses who had Aaron as his Wasi (legatee), Muhammad should have Ali his next in kin as Wasi. He started preaching his views in secrecy and gathered many followers who saw no leadership in Othman. When the network of this secret society was complete he moved and set his headquarter in Egypt with offshoot bases in Medina, Basra and Damascus. The group created several accusations—and fabrications—against

Othman: 1/he was weak and his assigned governors were corrupt, 2/ some of his aids and emirs are irreligious (Muawia for one) or inefficient, 3/ he permitted his regional emirs to adopt un-Islamic customs and practices from Persia and Byzantium, 4/ he appointed two emirs of his relatives opening a door to favoritism and, 5 / he mutilated the Koran while compiling it altering many verses and inventing new ones.

To heighten the pressure a mysterious letter was forged in the name of the poor Caliph to exterminate all followers of this move. It created a scandal of epic proportions. Before questioning Othman a group of armed insurgents surrounded his house. Othman asked Ali for help. Ali did not want a serious involvement knowing that Othman's days were numbered but in a zealous step assigned his two sons Hasan and Hussein to guard the house and left Medina. The insurgents entered from the backyard and assassinated Othman; one of them was Muhammad son of Abu Bakr! 'The Muslims refused to bury him in their cemetery and after his death two Muslims jumped on his dead body and broke one of his ribs.' (The Hidden Truth, page 25).

The death of Othman opened the Caliphate succession market to all soldiers of fortune. Only the most intelligent man in the lot, Muawia, whom Muhammad predicted earlier as "a future people's leader", was watching like a vulture from his Damascus vintage point. He ordered the bloody shirt of martyred Othman, a fellow Umayyad, and the cut fingers of his wife be sent to him at once. These will be his important future negotiating cards. The 'Shirt of Othman' became proverbial as is to this day when reviving hazy issues. From that day on the power struggle has been confined to Muawia and Ali.

Ali bin Abi Taleb, the short-lived fourth Caliph is the cousin of Muhammad, his son-in-low who married his daughter Fatima and the first man to embrace Islam. When he was 9 Muhammad asked him to move from his poverty-stricken paternal house to his mansion with Khadija. Ali pursued his Nazarene Ebionite education and like Muhammad, read, memorized and comprehended Waraka's Koran and acquired a special love to the written and spoken word. Soon enough he mastered the language and attained the highest degree in eloquence. His speeches, sermons and letters served for generations as models of spiritual and literary expression. His deep knowledge of the Mecca Koran that he virtually grew up with helped him put the book together under Abu Bakr and later add fresh same-style chapters to it under Omar and Othman.

Ali was saturated with the spirituality of the Bishop. Unlike Muhammad, politicking and warring did not rid him of the ascetic education that penetrated his soul as a kid. His book: "Nahj-ul-Balagha" matches the Koran in its eloquence and in many aspects outshines it in substance. A sample 'verse': "most men's demises (happen) under the lightning of greed." The book is comparable in the Bible to Solomon's book of Proverbs; while it enriches the mind with wisdom it deepens the spirit with mysticism. Perhaps Ali was the first Sufi in Islam; his disciples and descendents carried this flag after him. His atrocious assassination in the mosque assured his martyrdom, inviolability and eminence as Caliph and Imam. It is no wonder that some of such descendents, the Alawites, elevated him to deification. They ruled Syria since 1970 and are designated as "extremists—ghulat" and outside the bounds of Islam by the Muslim mainstream for such deification. Alawites believe in a system of divine incarnation as well as an esoteric reading of the Koran and regard Ali as the incarnation of the deity in a divine triad. This threesome is made of Ali or the "Meaning;" Muhammad or the "Name whom Ali created of his own light;" and Salman the Ebionite Persian as the "Gate."

Ali had another passion for swordsmanship and a great admiration to his valiant uncle Hamza who initiated him in the secrets of handling swords and defeating opponents. At 16 he was already an accomplished knight and swordsman. He devised for himself a special, twin-speared sword that became legendary in the battles he fought later with the Prophet. His Shia descendents today believe when Ali used to hit the ground with his Zul Fiqar (the twin-speared) earth would shudder down to its seventh layer!

But Ali's personality had many flaws. He was short and chubby, far imposing on a horse than on foot. He was astute in dealing with adversaries in battlegrounds but abysmal in handling people and situations: a great warrior and a dreadful manipulator; an always detached individual that never evoked credibility. This may have been the reason why Muhammad who bestowed on him great bravery titles and honors, did not proclaim him successor before his death. But Ali's zeal to Muhammad was unquestionable; his sword won critical battles and personally saved the Prophet in many perilous encounters.

Unfortunately Ali lacked realism in politics and governance. He was an ethereal man resorting to utopian theorizations rather than down-to-earth measures. He could not understand the basic needs and requirements of the new Empire like Omar did. He failed to formulate to his followers tangible plans and well defined objectives. The eloquence he used next to his sword was not always substantiated. In a speech to his Iraqi combatants he once said: "If I call you to fight them (the Damascene army of Muawia) in summer you would say it is too hot, in winter you would say too cold. Nobody knows wars better than I do. I started warring at 16 and I still do it at this age. But *he who is not obeyed cannot give orders*!" A pitiable plea indeed!

His followers today, the Shia, seem to pursue the same corridor of thinking and similar plight: they are great sacrificial victims for a given cause and rickety leaders when in power. Hence their reliance on a 'governance group' as is the case in Iran where no one takes any personal initiative. The Sunni, descendents of Mohammed's school and Umayyad Caliphate, adopt opposite tactics: no risk takers but leaders and clever manipulators. In Sunni Islam an Imam is simply a learned man who may lead prayers on Friday. Imams make no intercession with Allah for man as the Shia believe they do. As one cynic Sunni deftly put it: "for us Sunni it's direct dialing to God, the Shia go through the operator."

Perhaps the single, most devastating predicament in Ali's personal life was his intense sexuality. He was known to be unable to sleep one single night without copulation. At 45 he developed a big belly that further thwarted his personality. Besides Fatima and to her dismay he married countless women and fathered over 30 children. His own house was divided into many factions that in turn subdivided later and until this day among his followers.

It looks like Muhammad was always considering Ali as his kid warrior and servicing figurehead. He almost denied him the hand of his daughter Fatima in marriage. Ali fumed and ridiculed himself as a future leader when he went out publicly shouting and pestering Muhammad to impel him, despite Fatima's hesitation, into acquiescence. The Prophet changed mind. He was pleased later when Ali fathered two sons Hasan and Hussein; Muhammad grew very fond of them and relished them as his own male children that he was denied.

Ali was always a behind-the-scene man. He was dismayed when Abu Bakr and Omar hastened to conclude succession while he was preparing Muhammad's burial. When the spectacular act was apparent to him it was already a fait accompli; he simply missed the caravan. The same golden opportunity was lost when Omar appointed the counsel of six and Ali inexplicably pledged allegiance to Othman. Even after Othman's assassination he lost precious time away from troubled Medina instead of rallying supporters for his equitableand long awaited Caliphate. In fact it was the chief insurgent Malik Ushtar who first gave him the pledge of allegiance and when the other Companions were reluctant to do so Malik threatened them with his sword. Some of the Ansar (Muhammad's zealots in Medina) vacated the scene to avoid voting. Members of the Umayyad family fled to Damascus. The fourth Caliph in Islam could not garner any meaningful support for his rule. He accepted a Caliphate deal fraught with controversy. He had to wrangle his way through a precarious and unsuccessful rule that was ended by a merciful coup-de-grace: his assassination. The fearsome warrior but politically failing Imam acquired the martyrdom blessing and earned the reverence of his followers ever after.

Even before Othman's assassination subdivisions and splinter groups mushroomed all over the empire. One fanatical group called Khawarij (outsiders) appeared around in the fortieth year to Hijra and created a tidal wave within the Islamic state that still exists to this day. They claimed that Ali the uncertain Caliph, Muawia the ruler of Syria and Amr bin Al-As the ruler of Egypt, were not worthy to rule. Ali, to the intense pleasure of Muawia fought them at the Nahrawan battle to near annihilation. Their remnants soon regrouped and nicknamed all three 'the Imams of Mischief'. They maintained that the true Caliphate came to end with Omar and Muslims should govern themselves nowadays by the Book of Allah. They assigned three assassins to kill all three Imams in their mosques on one fixed night: 17 Ramadan. Muawia escaped death in Damascus thanks to his thick clothing in that cold winter morning; Al-As was also saved: the assassin mistook him for his police chief. Only Bin Muljam was lucky: he hit Ali on his face with a poisoned sword.

Muawia's cat-and-mouse playing with Ali did not culminate in any palpable victory. He was so elated in Damascus when he heard of Ali's death he set his failing assassin free! The Umayyad golden opportunity was wide open. Muawia, the shrewdest and most dedicated statesman in Islamic history finally tasted fortune; he skillfully maneuvered his way through the revolving door of religion and politics and braced with uncanny prescience to consolidate his empire stretching from India to the Atlantic shores.

ELEVEN

No Prophet
to his Country

"I do know you (Mecca) are the most beloved piece of all God's land to me. If it was not to the pagans who forced me out, I wouldn't have left you."

Muhammad

Muhammad was deeply disappointed when he began calling people to Islam in Mecca. The Majority of Meccans did not respond to his call. In this closely knit society where people know each other by name and thoroughly understand each other's history it was hard to admit that orphan Muhammad, the caravan tender suddenly turned into a prophet. They criticized him and called him mad (Koran 15.6), a possessed poet (Koran 37.36), a forger (Koran 16.101) and bewitched (Koran 25.7.8). They physically attacked him several times to harm or kill him. At one time a stone landed on his nose and front teeth breaking two of them irreparably. They persecuted his followers and pushed them to seclusion or exile in Abyssinia.

Either the Bishop underestimated the size of the task he put on Muhammad's shoulders or instead of straight admonition and sermonizing as Waraka endorsed Muhammad hastened to declare his prophethood on Abu Bakr's insinuation. The story of the night flight or "Israa" over the winged mule "Alburaq" from Mecca to Jerusalem and on the "Seventh Heaven" to meet Allah and his peers of prophets then land in Mecca before dawn added fuel to the fire. Nobody believed this "Midsummer Dream" and everybody dubbed it as a typical Muhammad hallucination. Their suspicion was further amplified when Abu Bakr himself confirmed: "I believe anything he says;" although the story caused him many ripples of concern.

At the outset of his call to Islam Muhammad followed Waraka's directives and spoke highly concerning the Jews and Nazarenes. He won all the Ebionite Nazarenes to his ranks but failed to win the Jews although he declared that Allah distinguished them above peoples and assigned governance of the (Palestine) land to them. The Koran says: "And verily we gave the children of Israel the scripture and the governance and the prophet hood and provided them with good things and favored them above all peoples" (Koran 45.16), and: "and when Moses said unto his people: O people! Remember Allah's favor unto you, how he placed among you prophets and he made you kings and he gave you what he gave not to any of his creatures. O my people! *Go into the holy land which Allah has ordained for you.*" (Koran 5.20,21).

Before Muhammad and Abu Bakr set out on 3 camels heading to Medina the latter sent notifying some of his Aws and Khazraj friends—and enemies of Quraish, of the Prophet's arrival. Aws and Khazraj thereafter called "Al-Ansar" or supporters were to Medina what Quraish was to Mecca. They shared the wealth of this agriculturally prosperous city along with few Jewish tribes prominent among them were: Qaynuqa and Nadir. The Khazraj set out a good show to the fleeing Prophet with their children carrying date branches and chanting salutation slogans with a refrain: "you have come with the obeyed command". This jovial access to the city was a re-enacting of Jesus' festive entrance into Jerusalem. In fact Al-Ansar bore intense hatred to prosperous and haughty Quraish and were on the lookout to challenge its authority. The arrival of Muhammad whose prophetic aura already reached them was anticipated and timely. His first move was to visit the tombs of his father and uncles, the second visit since he first came as a kid with his mother. It served to remind Al-Ansar that he was not that foreigner in their city and further helped his lording over Medina and dominating its supply routes and those of Mecca.

In the year 622 A.D. Muhammad asked his followers in Mecca and Abyssinia to make way in small numbers to Medina. As soon as he felt secure he started building his first Mosque with a modest adjacent house to which rooms were annexed later for his 12 wives. Slowly but steadily he established his small kingdom including a burgeoning army that was increasing with the conversion of Al-Ansar and the inflow of emigrants. He tried to win the Jews to his side and commanded Muslims to pray towards the destroyed Jewish temple in Jerusalem. He thought by this act the Jews would accept him as a true prophet. But they rejected his claim because he was an Arab who performed no miracles, uttered no prophecies and above all contradicted by his revelations the clear teachings of both the initial Mecca Koran and the Torah.

Dismayed, he changed the prayer direction from Jerusalem to the Qaaba in Mecca. It was a political move hailed by many Arabs without displeasing the Jews. He needed a revelation to do it and here it comes: "the fools among the people will say 'what has turned them from the Qibla (the direction to which the Muslims must turn when they pray) to which they were used? (Jerusalem) Say: To Allah belong both the East and the West: He guides whom He will to a way that is straight. We see the turning of your face [for guidance] to the heavens: now shall we turn you to a Qibla that shall please you (his intense love for Mecca). Turn then your face in the direction of the Forbidden Mosque: Wherever you are, turn your faces in that direction" (Koran 2:142); though the sacred mosque or Qaaba was full of idols at that time.

Muhammad was disgruntled. His troubled mind was telling him Islam is heading to stagnation and he is about to lose authority over his own followers. Day after day he found himself heeding Abu Bakr's implication to use the sword. He was reluctant in the beginning; Waraka's words for peaceful

Jihad still echo in his mind. "When the sword is once out among my followers it will be there till the Last Day" he said. It was apparent to him however that the Koran did not convince the Meccans, the other Christians (Tagleb) or the Jews. So he decided to pursue Abu Bakr's stratagem and use the sword. He went on preparing his army to the upcoming struggles with Quraish. As he and his growing followers needed food and other life sustenance, Medina was for him a strategic point to attack the Mecca-Damascus caravans and loot their precious loads. The raids intensified and inflicted tremendous loss to merchants including Abu Safian, holder of the flag and commander of Quraish's army, who redirected his caravans to the longer coastal route via Jeddah to avoid pilfering. He was dismayed Muhammad was practicing Jahiliya-style hit-and-run robbery attacks not befitting his claim as a prophet. He rallied Quraish and prepared for war.

Peaceful Jihad was the ultimate option first proclaimed by Waraka. This is now a big deviation to armed struggles. To convince his followers to fight he had to come up with fresh revelations heretofore inexistent in the Koran especially since many of them will have to fight against their own relatives in Mecca—against their fathers, brothers and even grandfathers. The revelation came in the following verses: "O Apostle, incite (literal translation) the believers to fight" (Koran 8.65). This command was further supported by a Torah story, the one of the children of Israel when they asked Samuel to appoint for them a king who became Saul. Zaid bin Thabet who did not possess Waraka's extensive knowledge took the stories of 'Gideon to bring to the water all the people who were gathered with him to fight so that God might test them', and

Samuel whom 'the children of Israel asked to appoint for them a king'. Zaid vaguely produced a similar recount: "fight in the way of Allah and know that Allah is Hearer, Knower . . ." and "bethink thee of leaders of the children of Israel after Moses, how they said unto a *Prophet whom they had*, set for us a king and we will fight in Allah's way. He said: would you then refrain from fighting if fighting were prescribed for you? They said: Why should we not fight in Allah's way when we have been driven from our dwellings with our children? Yet, when fighting was prescribed for them, they turned away all save a few of them. Allah is aware of evil-doers" (Koran 2.224). The simulation between the children of Israel who were *not* driven from their homes and families but rather commended by God to leave Egypt and the children of Quraish who were is inconsistent, yet brilliantly served the purpose.

Muhammad began to win battles over Quraish and his power increased. When the Muslims mourned because they killed their relatives in the Badr battle a comforting revelation came: "You slew them not, but Allah slew them. And you threw not when you did throw, but Allah threw, that he might test the believers by a fair test of Him. Lo! Allah is Hearer, Knower. (Koran 8:17).

Soon enough Muhammad convinced all Muslims that they were agents of Allah on earth. Their duty is to promote Islam first by intimation and failing that by force. Muhammad was elated with what the power of the sword already garnered him. It is recorded in Al-Tabari history that he declared in Medina: "I was sent by the sword. The good is with the sword, the good is in the sword, the good is by the sword. My followers will be always good as long as they carry the sword." To ensure that Muslims would fight to death they were promised "total forgiveness of any martyr's sins and eternal life in Paradise with wedded women of lovely eyes and rivers of milk and wine." (Koran 52: 17).

Furthermore, for Muslims to kill, crucify and cut hands and feet of those who do not believe in Islam was—and remains—a warranted behavior: "Fight them and Allah will torture them by your hands, disgrace them and you prevail over them" (Koran 9:14). And: "The only reward of those who make war upon Allah and His Messenger and strive after corruption in the land will be that they will be killed or crucified or have their hands and feet on alternate sides cut off or will be expelled out of the land. Such will be their degradation in the world and in the hereafter theirs will be in awful doom". (Koran 5:33). These Koranic verses purely incidental and directed at specific circumstances and individuals at the time they were revealed are still considered universal commandments and rules in Islamic countries. Naturally, terrorism proliferates as a by-product.

With their increased power the founding fathers decided to realize an old Quraish dream: exterminate the wealthy Jewish clans of Medina. They first expelled the tribe of Qainuqa then attacked Nadir and drove them out of town. Al-Ansar were very pleased and also wanted Bani Quraiza who sympathized with the Meccans during the battle of the Ditch. This clan suffered the worst fate: 700 of their men were slaughtered in one day; their women and children were enslaved. Muhammad also went after Nadir clan in neighboring fertile Khyber, yet on Abu Bakr's smart hint saved their necks against their yearly crop of wheat and grains and married their hostage Safia (Zainab later) wife of Kinana after he killed her husband and folks.

Muhammad decided to use force to subdue the Meccans and all those who opposed him. He did not forget those who harmed and harassed him before he left Mecca. He sent his zealots to exterminate them one by one. Terrors struck in Mecca and mellowed its inhabitants into submission. Muhammad then led his conquest on the city and when all Meccans gathered to greet his army he roared his victorious plea: "people of Mecca, what do you think I am doing with you?" "A generous brother and a bountiful cousin" they all retorted. "Go then, he told them, you are released" . . . Muhammad was back to his "most beloved town"; he was Quraish's hunted man and now he is the master. Abu-Safian himself, the staunchest enemy of Islam and commander of the Quraish armies on the battles of Badr and Ohud were granted a special concession: "Abu Safian is safe and whoever enters his house is safe".

One meaningful event is worth mentioning: Hind, the Damascene wife of Abu Safian and Mother of Muawia, had set up her Abyssinian servant and lance thrower to kill Hamza in the second battle of Ohud. Hamza had killed her two brothers earlier in Badr. When done, she rushed to the slain Hamza, extracted his liver with her knife and ate it! Her son Muawia by intimation of his shrewd father, was one of Muhammad's revelation scribes in Medina. Al-Ansar supporters were dismayed at Muhammad's lavishness to their Mecca enemies. They all realized they were the true Muslims but Quraish would be the actual rulers: "Faith in Medina and Governance in Mecca", they started propagating. Muhammad rushed to correct this oversight crediting and praising them and asking Allah to be kind to them in a pathetic and open plea until his shed tears washed down his beard!. That appeasing lip service did not change the fact that from now on his Quraish clan would reign over the peninsula and later on the Old World. Al-Ansar were merely tools in the grand design.

Perhaps one of the biggest controversies of Islam is that the would-be rulers, the Umayyad dynasty or Abu Safian descendents were no believers in Muhammad or Islam. Abu Safian who fought Muhammad on various battlegrounds joined Islam to reap the political fruits. Muhammad was always aware of his enmity that he later sent him from Medina a special "Saryia"—secret night killer—that failed to liquidate him. Ibn Hisham recorded that 'when the Prophet stood in Mecca to display the Muslim armies with all their banners, Abu-Sufian and Al-Abbas the prophet's uncle, stood to watch the parade. "The kingship of your nephew Muhammad became so great today" Abu-Sufian said to Al-Abbas. "It is the prophethood not the kingship, Abu-Sufian," Al-Abbas said. "As to prophethood I still have my reservations," Abu-Sufian answered.' (Islamic Caliphate, page 103). He later called on the day Othman was assassinated: "O sons of Umayya, catch it (Caliphate) as you catch a ball, by the one Abu Safian swears (!?) there will be no torture or judgment, paradise or hell, reincarnation or redemption". (Ibn Hisham).

This open agnosticism streamed down in the dynasty when the first Caliph Muawia married a Christian wife, employed the Christian poet Al-Akhtal and freely unleashed his tongue against Al-Ansar in Medina. Muawia,—another disconcerting phenomenon—was himself a companion and scribe to the

Prophet in Medina!? When his son and second Caliph Yazid took over he sent his Damascene army to subdue Medina. His commander, Alfahri, debauched its women to his soldiers for three days while Al-Ansar men fled away. This resulted of a new progeny of fair skins and blue eyes that still distinguish Medina's inhabitants today! He also ordered Hussain, son of Ali who challenged his authority in Iraq killed and his head sent to Damascus on a spear. Yazid held the head before a Damascene gathering and went tapping on the teeth with his gold stick and reciting a piece of his poetry that rhymes as well in English:

> There were no inspirations, nor revelations
> Simply Hashemite kingship manipulations
> If I do not revenge, call me not Umayyad
> For all those misdeeds* inflicted by Muhammad

*In reference to his killed relatives in the battle of Badr.

Further down to Caliph Alwaleed Bin Yazeed who ruled the Muslims in the year 743 A.D. and who replicated the saying about Muhammad of old Abu Sufian in the following verses: (Talaaba bin nobowati Hashimioun—Fala wahion ataho wala kitabo) or:

> "A Hashemite manipulated prophet hood
> —with no revelation upon him or a book."

He used to shoot a large copy of the Koran made of deer hide with arrows until holes covered it. Then he wrote a poem addressed to the Koran saying: "In the Day of Judgment, when Allah asks you: Who made all these holes in you? Say: Alwaleed did that" (The Hidden Truth, 86).

It is also reported that Abdul Malik Bin Marwan, whose Umayyad Empire stretched from the Iberian Peninsula West to the borders of China East had the Koran on his lap when he was installed. After he became Caliph he folded the Koran and said "this is the last time I will ever see you." (Islamic Caliphate-History).

If one considers that a Caliph is the Imam of all Muslims who solemnly leads the five daily prayers in mosques it becomes clear that the Medina Islam was a means to achieve political ends more than a faith to lift the souls. The twisted, multi-faceted doctrine could only be straightened if supported by a military triumph or martyrdom as in the case of Hussein who faced far superior odds and was killed in battle at Karbala in 680AD. His Shia followers see in him the ultimate martyr and celebrate his death with so intense and bloody passion that is sometimes deadly. They see his descendents of contemporary imams holding power on earth until the 12th imam, the Awaited Mahdi, returns to earth at a time unknown. Shortly before his death Hussain said in a poem:

Should Muhammad's faith be straightened out
Only by killing me . . . O swords, wipe me out . . .

TWELVE

The Death of Muhammad

*"Say: I have no power over any good or
harm on myself except as Allah wills. If I
had knowledge of the unseen, I should have
multiplied all good, and no evil should have
touched me: I am but a warner . . ."*

Koran 7:188.

The final days of Muhammad arrived. He had gained
control over the Arabian Peninsula and established
Mecca as the only holy shrine to be acknowledged.

He canceled Jerusalem and reverted to the Qaaba as an inspirational prayer beacon.

In the tenth year after Hijra Muhammad made his farewell pilgrimage to Mecca. Soon after his return to Medina he fell ill. At least the one verse above in the Koran alludes to his death. Clerics refer to his terminal ailment by a simple word: "pain". In fact he was poisoned by the only long-term lethal toxin known in those days: iron dioxide. The same toxin administered later to Napoleon in Santa Helena. It happened when Khyber was conquered. Here is the story:

"Zainab bint Al-Hareth, wife of the poet Salam bin Mishkam went about asking which part of the lamb was Muhammad's favorite. People told her, "It is the upper front leg for it is the best and farthest from harm." She slaughtered a lamb and took the deadly poison and poisoned the animal putting more on the shoulders. Before sunset when women hostages paraded in front of Muhammad he threw his clock on Safya (whom he married later) and took her to his tent. After prayer, Zainab was sitting at his feet and she said, "O Abu al-Qasem, here is a gift I have for you." Muhammad ordered his friends to take it from her and it was put before him and his friends for dinner. Among them was Bishr bin Marur. Muhammad said, "Come near and be seated". He took the leg and ate as well as Bishr. When Muhammad swallowed his bite, Bishr swallowed his. Muhammad suddenly said, "Raise your hands; this leg and this shoulder tell me they are poisoned." Bishr said, "By the one who honored you I found the same in my morsel but when you ate that which was in your mouth, I did not desire my soul more than yours and I would not spoil the pleasure of your food." A part of the lamb was thrown to a dog and the dog died. Bishr's color turned black and his pain lasted two years after which he died."

Then Muhammad sent for this Jewess and asked her, "Have you poisoned this lamb?" She said, "You have acquired certain powers with which you judge those who are not loyal to you. You killed my father, my uncle and my brother . . . So I said, "If he is a king then I would be relieving us of him and if he is a prophet he will be able to perceive." It was said he pardoned her while others claim he ordered her crucified. When Muhammad fell ill just before his death he said to his youngest wife, "Aisha, I still feel the effect of that poisoned food I ate; this is the time of my demise by that poison." When Bishr's sister entered his room during his last sickness he said to her, "this is the time of my demise by the meal I ate with your late brother in Khaiber." (Ibn Hisham & Sahih Bokhari).

"When the Prophet was expiring, surrounded by men among them Omar Bin Al-Khattab he said: "let me write you a testimonial by which you will never later go astray". Omar (immediately discerned he may utter something concerning the Caliphate of his cousin Ali) harshly prompted everybody, "The Prophet is overwhelmed by his pain. You all have the Koran, the book of Allah is enough for us." (Sahih Bokhari-History). By his decisive interference, Omar cut short the possibility for Muhammad to name Ali as his successor. Followers of Ali today hate Omar as they do the devil to the point that throughout Iran and the Shia of Iraq, the Gulf and Lebanon no newborn may be named Omar; a very common name among Sinna.

Before Muhammad passed away he summoned Abu Bakr, Omar, Othman and Ali, and directed them to see "that there will be no two religions in the Arabian Peninsula". This final command was shortly fulfilled by Omar. It reverberates to our days where in Saudi Arabia for instance no church could be erected for expatriates to worship; it is also the fundamentalists' divine ammunition to insist on casting the infidels out of the Peninsula.

Finally on June 632, death came to Muhammad in the room of his wife Aisha as he rested on her lap. He was 64 years old. Aisha was only 16!

THIRTEEN

Queries on the Koran

"It is a Koran in Arabic, for people who understand."
Koran—various

The Koran used by Muslims today is a consolidated document of three main consecutive works, two of them appeared during the life of Muhammad and one was amended and modified later by Othman. The Koran takes great care to outline the common monotheistic heritage of Judaism and Christianity but works equally hard to distinguish Islam by mentioning exclusively Arabian *prophets* like Hud, Salih, Shu'ayb, Luqman and others to remind readers that it is "A Koran in Arabic, for people who understand." Despite its repeated assertions to the contrary the Koran is often extremely difficult for contemporary readers to understand even by highly educated speakers of Arabic. It sometimes makes dramatic shifts in style, tone, and subject matter from one verse to another and assumes a familiarity with language, stories and events that seems to have been lost even to the earliest of Muslim exegetes: a typical text that initially evolved in the oral tradition.

Under the Abbasid Caliph al-Ma'mun (813-833), an influential group known as Mu'tazila (the secluded, mentioned earlier in this book) developed a complex theology based partly on a metaphorical rather than simply literal understanding of the Koran. By the end of the tenth century the influence of the Mu'tazila school had waned for complicated political reasons and the official doctrine had become that of *i'jaz* or the "inimitability" of the Koran (the Bridge of Eloquence). As a result the Koran has traditionally not been translated by Muslims for non-Arabic-speaking Muslims. Instead it is read and recited in the original by Muslims worldwide whose majority does not speak Arabic. The translations that do exist are considered to be nothing more than scriptural aids and paraphrases. The adoption of the doctrine of inimitability was another drive to further rule out men's minds in the textual Koran and a major turning point in Islamic history. From the tenth century to this day the mainstream Muslim understanding of the Koran as the literal and uncreated Word of God has remained constant. To cover an overall clarification of its various phases we shall discuss:

the Mecca Koran, the Medina Koran, the Othman Koran as well as the contradictory aspects of the book . . .

The Mecca Koran as we have seen was the original compilation of the Ebionite Mathews Gospel from the Aramaic language in a highly lyrical and rhetorical style. The most important guidelines of faith are still as originated. The presence of Ebionites in Mecca who were first to embrace Islam as a continuance of their own faith pronounced in Arabic, presumes the existence of the Aramaic "Gospel according to Hebrews" in their hands. The same book Waraka rewrote "in a clear Arabic tongue". That was the only Gospel Ebionite Waraka dealt with although at the time of Muhammad many other gospels were there in the hands of Christian factions like the Nestorian tribe of Tagleb.

The translation that took place was not literal the way we understand it today. It was in fact what is best described by the Arabian Koran itself: "detailing," "replication," "easiness" and "admonition." This old procedure was adopted to bring foreign thoughts into locally accepted textual forms.

The Koran means "Kira'a" or reading from the Aramaic verb "Karou". It was written in rhymed Arabic language from the 'Original Book': "We have made it an Arabic Koran so you may be able to understand, it is in the *Mother of the Book* with us, high and full of wisdom." (Koran 43:3). It also says: "Had we sent this in a foreign language (Aramaic version) they would have said: why are not the verses explained in details . . ." (Koran 41:44). 'Explained in details' meant translated into Arabic and detailed into chapters. It was done with flowing easiness so the Prophet—and his followers—would read and memorize with no great difficulty: "We have not given you the Koran for your distress, but only an admonition to those who fear." (Koran 20:2).

The question of direct and literal revelation from God needs further clarification. Muhammad was well aware of the revelation continuity between the Hebrew Gospel and its Arabic "Kara'a". The fresh inspiration he received came to him as it came before him: "We have sent you inspiration as we sent it to Noah and the messengers after him . . ." (Koran 4:163). "Inspiration" is not necessarily a dictation of an idea but an insinuation thereof. The Koran repeats in many instances "Revelation on you and those before you". So if the revelation on Muhammad is a recurrence of the old ones, the same inspiration remains in essence in the Arabian Koran and *the same one in the "previous Book" or the "Mother of Books"*. All followers, Kitabi or Ummi, should believe in both previous and detailed books: "Those deeply rooted in knowledge (Nazarenes) among them and the believers (other Arabs), believe in what has been revealed to you (Koran) and what was revealed before you (Torah and Gospel)." (Koran 4:162).

Mathew's Gospel fitted well into Waraka's Ebionite conviction and principles not only in pursuing Jesus' doctrines but those of Torah as well. On the other hand the Koran itself referred solely to the Aramaic Gospel in three or more letter codes that the 'Skillful Erudite' Waraka, probably mindful of any possible discrediting after him, inserted at the beginnings of his Mecca chapters (Suras). These remain today and forever constant and unalterable parts of the original manuscript. Examples:

1/ 'A.L.R.' (Koran—Hood and other chapters).
In reference to the three Aramaic words: 'Amar Li Rabo' meaning: 'thus directed me God'.

2/ 'A.L.M.' (Koran—many other chapters)
In reference to the three Aramaic words: 'Amar Li Morio' meaning: 'thus asked me the Lord'

Muslim interpreters of the Koran today are apparently at a loss to decipher these codes. They refer to them as: "Allah alone knows His intention". In fact these codes who were first in the Hebrew Gospel and later in the Koran invariably precede a heavenly reference to the importance of the book: 'A.L.R. a Book whose verses were well defined, then segmented by a skillful erudite' (Koran, Hood Chapter). This indicates that the Koran was inspired by a holy testament that Ebionites believe it was inspired by God to Mathew and 'defined then segmented (translated) by a skillful erudite'. This is this assumption that gave the Koran the revelation characteristics.

The word 'Sura' means more than a chapter. It connotes a state of vehemence, severity and spell. All three conditions characterized the state of trance or frenzy a human may be subjected to when receiving a revelation. Sura is also used in Arabic to denote states of anger, intense pleasure or ensuing fight. The word was used for the Koran chapters to distinguish them as awe-inspiring texts apart from other worldly documents.

In fact both Waraka and Muhammad were proud and elated of the Koran achievement: "Say: if the whole of mankind and Jinn were to rally together to produce the like of this Koran they could not produce the like thereof, even if they backed up each other with help and support" (Koran 17:88). This challenge though was met several times before and after Waraka when it comes to poetic eloquence. In the age of Jahilyia before Muhammad there were men who produced the like of the Koran. Even at the time Islam was burgeoning, Muslima of Yamama (Riyadh today) came up with a similar book which was immediately destroyed along with the writer and all his supporters. By the end of the Abbasid dynasty the famous poet Mutanabi (nickname for 'Prophesier') claimed prophecy, produced a comparable Koran and was imprisoned. Even in our modern times the "Mus'haf" of Duruz, a Muslim sect with a different Islamic approach through reason (see Chapter 21), is an undisclosed book that rivals the Koran's style and expressiveness.

The Bishop and the Prophet certainly achieved together an impressive series of accomplishments. The first success of Waraka is his choosing Muhammad; dislocating him from his impoverished milieu, marrying him to Khadija and training him for twenty years to learn, assimilate and contemplate. The second success is in decoding the Hebrew Gospel into a moving and mind boggling poetic prose creating the basic Koran. The third achievement is rallying under Islam the various Nazarene factions dispersed in the Hijaz as one nation under one religion, a faith of 'unison' merging the Book, the factions and Allah: "there is no God but Allah'.

Nazarenes in the Meccan Koran were the first and real Muslims among other Arabs. They were an exemplary support to Muhammad. He would consult them, praise their backing, respect their monks and confer with them on the authenticity of his message: "those who received God's guidance; copy the guidance they received . . ." (Koran 6:90). Nazarenes testify on the validity of what he came up with: "those deeply rooted in knowledge among them and the believers, believe in what was revealed to you . . ." (Koran 4:162). He esteemed their clerics describing them as, "repenting, servants, praising and devotees; they bow down and prostrate themselves in prayer . . ." (Koran 9:112). He clearly distinguished between them and the Jews who did not respond to his message, "Strongest among men in enmity to the believers will you find the Jews and the Pagans (Quraish). And nearest among them in love to the believers will you find those who say we are Nazarenes . . ." (Koran 5:82).

This Meccan Koran was the one Muhammad read and memorized than started to preach, sermonize and educate. He was propagating the word of God with personal conviction and unshaken faith. He taught people the book and the wisdom and enlightened them with the previous scriptures of Moses and Jesus all within his prescribed titles of 'Messenger,' 'Admonisher' and 'Warner'. At that stage people should not question nor examine the role of their man, it is a clean and well defined mission: he is simply a *man* among them: "Is it a matter of wonderment that we sent our inspiration to a man among them to warn people and give the good news to the believers." (Koran 10:2).

The Meccan Koran was not written in one volume but scattered on palm leaves, hides, stones and cattle skins and disseminated in parts to believers. It had no chapters or 'Suras.' Muhammad was confined within this framework for the first 3 years after announcing his mission. Then

Khadija and Waraka died and a brand new Islam ensued. The 'Prophet' replaced the 'Messenger' and fresh, incidental revelations of the same style and approach were added to the book at random. The purpose was to face, contain or repel arising contingencies.

The multifaceted structure of the Koran and the many versions it appears under is further compounded by the seven different ways of expressions. The difference between those versions was not in meaning but in words like using grace and gracefulness, possessions and properties etc . . . In fact the difference between those seven versions was meant to give full flexibility to many interpretations. Hence today the Koran entails 'Ulums' or sciences for its interpretation; the specialized clerics in such fields are called 'Ulemas'. Those differ from Sinna (Muhammad and his followers' sayings but not Ali's), and Shia (Mohammad's and Ali's sayings with emphasis on Ali). The latter established much more sophisticated 'Hawzas' centers of advanced theologies based mostly on both sayings plus those of Ali's martyred son Hussein and the descendent Imams.

The Medina Koran that complemented the first book altered the original substance, connotations and to the keen observer, style. It shifted from the spiritual compassion of Mecca to the authoritarian condescension of Medina. It even contained many language and grammatical mistakes that later, Hajjaj bin Yusuf, governor of Iraq and language authority corrected many of them. It came piecemeal according to the events and occasions. Revelations started seeping after a long period of drainage since the death of Waraka from whom Muhammad inherited enough religious ammunition to go by. Medina requisites were different; while the Meccan Koran contended with the basic belief directives, Medina requirements involved supportive issues to the raids, conquests and various war eventualities. Islam shifted here from Koranic verses to sword strikes. This swing generated fresh stances, contradicting attitudes and fanatic militancy. The wars against Quraish then against the Jews and later against the Christians at large necessitated revelations condemning all and inciting followers to fight them.

The praise and appreciation bestowed on the Jews, their books and prophets in the Meccan Koran as in this verse: "How can they choose you as a judge when they have the Torah, which contains God's judgment . . . We had sent down the Torah containing guidance and light," (Koran 5:43), provided a clear indication it was not necessary for the Jews to go to Muhammad for judgment having it all in the Torah guidance and light. All that changed suddenly to ruthless condemnations in Medina: "fight against such of those who have been given the scriptures (Jews and Christians) *as believe not in Allah* nor the Last Day (?), and forbid not that which Allah has forbidden by His Messenger (Muhammad) and follow not the religion of truth (Islam), until they pay tribute (taxes) with willing submission while suppressed." (Koran 9:29). This verse established forever that Jews and Christians living in Islamic countries are to be treated as second class citizens paying high taxes to upkeep their faiths. Under the most advanced Islamic civilization of the Abbasid, Jews and Christians were branded: forced to wrap a red cloth around their waists as an identifying mark.

The plight of any Muslim today who takes the Koran literally is how to refrain from the fundamentalism these fiery verses are dragging him into. His clerics who diffidently maintain that their book is 'effective for any time and place' shall not venture to say that such verses were confined to specific times and circumstances therefore inappropriate and outdated. These verses constitute a dangerous arousal to fanatics like Abu Hafs Al-Mesri who declared on a prime time T.V. program in London that 'even though he carries the British nationality his duty as a Muslim is to fight 'Jihad' the British in their country to promote Islam.' Otherwise he won't be a good Muslim. The majority of Muslims share this belief but follow the Prophet's adage, "be hushed until you have the upper hand."

More verses demonstrate that Medina's Islam was heading to an Islamic empire, "say to the infidels (literally) if they desist from unbelief, their past would be forgiven them; but if they persist the punishment of those before them is a warning to them. And fight them until there is no more sedition (literally) and Islam becomes Allah's in its entirety." (Koran 8:38). The Founding Fathers of the upcoming empire were clearly in control manipulating the Prophet—as Omar did on his death bed—to pursue their charted course. The Medina Koranic revelations were there to set the new record straight.

Zaid bin Thabet became literate in some Hebrew, Aramaic and old Judeo-Christian scriptures that Muhammad asked to fill him in, proved to be lacking in that trade. He entangled the Prophet in many uncertainties. Baseless attacks aimed at Jews and Christians' inherited belief started trickling. The Medina Koran says, "The Jews Call Uzair a son of Allah and the Christians call Christ the son of Allah. That is saying from their mouths; they but imitate what the infidels (literal) of old used to say. Allah's curse be on them; how they are deluded away from the truth." (Koran 9.30). The name Uzair here is a derivative of the Pharaohs god Osiris whom the Hebrews never took on in their Scriptures. Throughout the gory struggle against the Jews nothing was spared to alienate them from the believers. The Koran says, "O ye who believe, take not the Jews—and the Christians—as partisans. They are but partisans to each other. And who among you befriends any of them, becomes one of them (infidel)." (Koran 5:51).

This command of the Koran was ignored many times through history when it comes to power, politics and money. In modern times the Gulf States did not hesitate to appeal to Christian nations to protect them from an Iraqi invasion led by Saddam Hussein who had a Koran copy written with his blood and who claimed lineage to the Prophet. The Prophet's Hadis however provide them with a Fatwa that warrants this practice, "Blessed He who enslaved *this* to us that we did not anticipate". Muslims still believe when they work with infidels that Allah subjugated these for their service even when it comes to Muslims very life saving from hunger or calamities. In Saudi Arabia today the relationship between a non-Muslim employee and his employer is covertly that of a slave and master.

When Abu Bakr took over the Caliphate many of those who had memorized the Koran died while fighting the apostates in the battle of Yamama, whose chief was Muslima, a same-time competitor to Muhammad ridiculed later as 'Musailima (little Muslima) the Imposter.' Omar feared that the death of those men would result in the loss of a great portion of the Koran and suggested to Abu Bakr that the Koran should be collected in one volume. "Abu Bakr was reluctant since Muhammad himself did not do it during his life. Authoritarian Omar persuaded him to do so. Abu Bakr ordered none other than Zaid bin Thabet to do the Job." (Almus'haf-history). Bin Thabet exclaimed: 'by Allah if they ordered me to shift one of the mountains it would not have been heavier for me than this order to collect the Koran. Then I said to Abu Bakr, "how will you do something that Allah's Apostle did not do?" Abu Bakr said, "By Allah it is a good thing". (Ibn Hisham—Historian).

Zaid was right in his assumption. When Islam shifted from a spiritual move to armed incursions and became the religion of many countries each group used the version that was known among them; the Syrians adopted Abi Kaab's version, the people in Kofa (Iraq) read bin Massoud's version, others took Abu Moussa Ashari's version and so on. Zeid spent the full span of Abu Bakr/Omar's Caliphates collecting verses from hundreds of sources all over the empire without reaching an acceptable format. Upon Omar's constant follow up and bullying on him he would apologize every time and promise to renew his efforts.

The Othman Koran was therefore in the offing. When Othman became Caliph he was confronted by much confusion wherein the sedition was brewing. He ordered Zeid bin Thabet again, assisted by three other Prophet Companions from Quraish: Alzubair, Aluss and Ibn Hisham (the authority quoted frequently in this book). His first recommendation to them: "if you disagree in anything in the Koran write in the language of Quraish because the Koran *was first revealed in the language of Quraish.*" (Al-Mus'haf—history).

Dr. Taha Hussain the 'Pillar of Arabic Literature' and former minister of education in Egypt, described that tumultuous process in his book (the Great Sedition): "Prophet Muhammad said: 'the Koran was revealed in seven dialects all of them are right and perfect.' When Othman *banned whichever he banned* from the Koran and *burned whichever he burned*, he banned passages Allah has revealed and burned parts of the Koran which were given to Muslims by the Messenger himself. He appointed a small group of Sahaba (Prophet's companions) to rewrite the Koran and left out those who heard Muhammad and memorized what he said. This is why Ibn Massoud (a trusted companion and historian also quoted in this book) was angry because he was one of the best men who memorized the Koran. He said that he took from the mouth of the Prophet himself seventy Suras of the Koran at a time Zeid bin Thabet was yet a young lad. When Ibn Massoud publicly objected to the burning of the other codices of the Koran Othman forced him out of the mosque and struck him to the ground breaking one of his ribs."

Why much of the original Koran was burnt while other parts were rewritten? Why did Othman attempt to mutilate a book that was "nay, this is a glorious Koran in a *Tablet Preserved?*" The answers are obvious and available:

When the Prophet died his followers split up into various factions. "Some said he did not die; Allah elevated him up as he did Jesus. They quarreled about his burial place: the Meccans wanted him in Mecca while Al-Ansar insisted on

Medina, others suggested he should be buried in Jerusalem."
(Baghdadi—Historian). Sectarian conflicts swelled to involve
many nations conquered with their religions wiped out. The
conquerors did not distinguish between Jews and Christians,
Persians and Romans, believers or pagans. Jihad in the way of
Allah became now Jihad after "many gains they will acquire,"
(Koran 48: 19) that "Allah promised them to acquire." (Koran
48. 20). Had it been really 'in the way of Allah' they would
have differentiated between conquests to disseminate Islam
and conquests to garner wealth and political supremacy with
careful delineation between subjugated peoples.

Othman's Koran redirected Muslims to handle the
vanquished, support the victors and fight to submission those
who opposed their expansion or renounced their call. Several
verses were added or altered to support feuding clans or justify
conquerors' misdeeds. Thus the Othman Koran was filled with
contradicting stances and newly picked legislations. It lost
conformity and language consistency inherent to the Meccan
Koran. Most of the contradictions targeted the Christians. We
will illustrate some of the changes: in this age where the 'Clash
of Civilizations" percolates like a new cold war; it could be a
constructive stride towards possible appeasement.

Othman's Koran did not distinguish the Nazarenes who
were different from Jews and Christians alike. These did not
deny the prophecy of Jesus nor did they claim he was the Son
of God. They were "a middling nation" (Koran 2:143) on
whose belief Islam was conceived to create another "middling
nation." These same early Islam supporters were accused
as any Christians in and outside the Peninsula of 'Shirk'
(worshipping the triune God) and simply branded as infidels.

While the Mecca Koran praised their clergy, Othman's accused them of "fabricating their monasticism themselves,' (Koran 57:27) and their priests who "in falsehood devour the substance of people," (Koran 9:34) and "they take their priests and their anchorites to be their lords in derogation of God." (Koran 9:31).

Othman threw the word 'Christians' in each verse originally addressed to Jews creating obvious misconceptions. In Medina, Muhammad had his major conflicts with Quraish and the Jews but none with the Christians because only a handful of them were there. Examples: "They say: "be Jews or Christians and you would be guided," (Koran 2:135), inserting—or Christians—blemishes the original rhyme of the verse (kono hoodan tahtado). Another example: "Or do you say that Abraham, Ismail, Isaac, Jacob and the tribes were Jews or Christians?" (Koran 2:140). Christianity took place much later for these prophets to be named Christians; other verses before and after this one were all addressed to Jews: "Abraham was not a Jew or a Christian but he was in true faith . . ." (Koran 2.67), etc . . .

The two main justifications of such radical alterations were first the military successes achieved by the conquerors in many countries with mixed ethnicities and the need for simplistic and homogenous legislations to perform governance without superfluous details, and second to subdue the countless Arab Christian communities well established in Syria, Iraq, Palestine and Lebanon much earlier than Islam's proclamation; a clear recurrence of the Tagleb tribulation. The only straightforward approach was to consider all non-Muslims as infidels. To alleviate the edgy tone of this term a worse yet milder word was introduced: 'Zummi', meaning infidels who pay tribute and live under Muslim protection.

The mix-up between the original Mecca Koran and Othman's was tremendous: transfers of Meccan verses into Medina chapters and vice versa; chapters listed in descending format according to the length of each irrespective of timely occurrence, location or reasons for revelation. Criticism did arise. As Muslims increasingly came into contact with Christians during the eighth century wars of conquest were accompanied by theological polemics in which Christians and others latched on to the confusing literary state of the Koran as proof of its human origins. Many of those even challenged the authenticity of Islam all together: "Can it be possible that so many creatures have lived and died for something that may be regarded as a tragic fraud?" wondered among many others Thomas Carlyle himself. Muslim scholars were fastidiously cataloguing the problematic aspects of the Koran, unfamiliar vocabulary, seeming omissions of text, grammatical incongruities, deviant readings and so on. A major theological debate in fact arose within Islam in the late eighth century pitting those who believed in the Koran as the "uncreated" and eternal Word of God against those who believed in it as created and manmade.

So when Westerners talk about Islam by quoting the early "revelations" or the Mecca Koran they are not communicating the truth about fundamentalist Islam portrayed throughout the Medina Koran but are actually inoculating and misleading those within their spheres of influence against the true nature of Islam. No doubt a few Muslim scholars have tried to negate the Medina "annihilate the infidel" passages but their arguments are weak, unconvincing and considered non-mainstream to the most vocal and influential scholars throughout the world.

The "Othman Koran" challenged history and tore down its principles. It was imposed on people forcibly; all other codices were irretrievably destroyed. Othman's tampering was later witnessed and condemned by Aisha herself who was the best among all Muhammad's wives in memorizing the book as she started on it with her sharp memory of a kid-wife: "Surat Al-Ahzab, she said after Othman's demise, was a 200-verse chapter during the prophet's life; when Othman rewrote the Koran it became what is now (only 72)." (The Legend and the Heritage, page 274).

Today's Muslims are unknowingly divided into two major factions: the mild and moderate who follow the docile teachings of the Mecca Koran with its scattered verses still distinctly discernible throughout the book and the fundamentalists who pursue the Medina texts overlooking the reconciliatory verses of Mecca. The Medina Koran shuffled all the papers and undermined the early mission of Muhammad who once predicted: "my nation is moving from prophethood to Caliphate and thence to a sinister empire". The Othman Koran opened all doors to contradicting opinions, revived the old and created new splinter groups instilled by all types of radicalisms. Muslims' divisions to Sunna and Shia, Ansar and Emigrants, Hashemite and Umayyad, Quraishi and Arabs, people of the House (Muhammad and Ali) and people of the Faith (Medina clans) all relatively quelled in Muhammad's lifetime suddenly surfaced after his death. The initial cause was the Prophet's failure to determine his successor as Waraka and later Abu Bakr did; secondly, the spiritual mission of Mecca was dissolved in Medina's warring theatre; its righteous book was assimilated by Medina's legislative one and later partially abrogated by Othman.

Unfortunately Muslims today are more attached to the prevailing Othman book, symbol of their glorious victories and conquests rather than to the overwhelmed Mecca Koran; although the latter advocates the 'Right Faith' of Abraham who was 'a unifier, devout and Muslim'. With the reshuffled Othman product in their hands they are unable to tell the two scriptures apart which could be one of the purposes behind Othman's performance: his Koran specifies the Suras by 'Meccan and Medinan' under which all verses are jumbled irrespective of origins. To tell them apart only intuition and good sense will help.

Contradictory aspects therefore abound in the Koran due to the many interfering hands and pens that alternated throughout its compilation and the various circumstances that necessitated the revelation of specific verses. Its apparent inconsistencies are easy to find: God may be referred to in the first and third person in the same sentence; divergent versions of the same story are repeated at different points in the text; divine rulings occasionally contradict one another. In this last case the Koran anticipates criticism and defends itself by asserting Allah's right to abrogate its own message "Allah does blot out or confirm what He pleases."

This multi-faceted book seemingly devoid of logic provides endless aspects of generalizations. One noted theologian, Imam Yahia bin Hussain says: "figure out that the Koran is both distinct and amorphous, revealed and verbalized, copier and copied, private and public, allowed and disallowed, definite and infinite; its beginning is like its end, the familiar is like the unfamiliar . . . streamlined and *devoid of contradictions*". (Bedaya & Nehaya.) This is in itself a contradictory masterpiece on paradoxes the besieged Muslim mind can only afford but to accept!

To explicate and justify the many inconsistencies most clerics interpret the Koran by the principle of *nasikh*, meaning that later passages supersede earlier ones or totally negate them. The Arabic words *nasikh* and *mansukh* derive from the same root verb *nasakha* which carries meanings such as "abolish, replace, withdraw and abrogate." The *nasikh*, an active participle, is "the abrogating," while *mansukh*, passive, means "the abrogated." In technical language *mansukh* refers to certain parts of the Koranic revelation that have been "abrogated". In other words to fundamentalist Muslims the most virulent passages of their sacred text have the right of way.

To further justify inconsistencies resulting from the enormous shuffles the Koran declares that Allah caused some of his revelations to be abrogated and some to be forgotten and in that case He gave better or similar revelations: "none of Our revelations do We abrogate or cause to be forgotten, but We substitute something better or similar: did not you know that Allah has power over all things? (Koran 2:106). To this very date Muslims refer their inexplicable theories to Allah; their clerics provide their best assiduity in explaining a religious conjecture touching their livelihood but end their inconclusive presentations with 'Allah A'alam' (Allah knows more). In fact the Muslim belief attributes perfection only to God. Man should not attain absolute perfection in anything he writes or even manufactures as he would be defying Allah. Have you been told how to pick up a genuine hand-made Iranian carpet? There is always a fault—an intended fault—somewhere in its intricate ornaments to make it imperfect. It would be a blasphemy if perfection is inherent to man!

The Koran came 600 years after Christ; its basic commandment to Muslims was to maintain the mandates of the Torah and the Gospel; yet many of its contents disagree with the records of these two books for four main reasons: 1/ many of the words were picked not to serve the meaning but to fit the all-important rhyme and rhythm. 2/ In transcribing the Bible stories Waraka did not go into minute details for fear that the Arab mind will not digest them, 3/ Bin Thabet in Medina was not qualified enough for factual translations from Hebrew and Aramaic, and 4/ The Koran perpetuated many pre-Islamic era (Jahiliya) myths and fables that remain today at the core of Islamic belief. A couple of examples on each instance will illustrate:

1a. The Koran says: "Read in the name of your Lord who creates; creates man from a clot." (Koran 96:1). The word 'Alaq' or 'clot' was picked to rhyme with 'Khalaq' or 'create'. Man has not been created from a frozen blood or whatever interpreters explain the meanings of 'clot'.

This is contradicted—or corrected—in the following verses: "Behold, my Lord said to the angels: 'I am about to create man from clay . . .'" (Koran 38:71).

1b. In the Chapter of Mary it says: "She said 'I seek refuge from you to God if you were 'Taqiya'." (Koran 19:18). To some clerics 'Taqiya' literally means 'pious'. To others it is a bad man's name. If 'pious' were meant Mary wouldn't seek refuge from him to God. The other clerics are right; a man's name was picked at random to fit other rhymes in the Sura: 'Sabiya, Sawiya, etc . . .

2a. the stories of Zachariah, Mary, Abraham, Ismail, Job and Lot, save some details on Zachariah and Mary were mere hints without much details. The purpose was to refer followers to the Bible with fresh, easily grasped narratives, no matter how distant in substance from the origin.

2b. "And We revealed the Gospel to Jesus and reinforced Him with the Holy Spirit . . ." and, "We revealed the Torah to Moses . . ." (Koran: various verses). The Koran and all Muslims insist that the Torah and Gospel were revealed verbatim to Moses and Jesus to justify the 'Koran revelation on the illiterate Prophet.' They are not ready to agree these were books written by humans to record the history and statements of the Prophets and those who followed them. They maintain these books are grossly manipulated and a far cry from the original "Revealed Books." This is a big obstacle in any rapprochement 'dialogue' in the future.

3a. The Koran is a constant reminder to upkeep the Torah and Gospel teachings yet all stories copied thereof are inaccurate: "And Mary the daughter of Imran, who guarded her vagina (literal) and we breathed into it of our spirit . . ." (Koran 66:12). And: O sister of

Aaron . . ." (Koran 19.28). In fact Mary, mother of Jesus was not Mary the daughter of Imran or the sister of Aaron. The difference in time between the two Marys is more than 1300 years. The mother of Jesus was from the tribe of Judah, the sister of Aaron from the tribe of Levi. When this controversy is argued with Muslim clerics they resort to two explanations: 1/ "sister of Aaron" is used figuratively to denote piety and/or 2/ the Torah was mutilated.

3b. Hundreds of years before Copernicus and Galileo the Torah declared that planet earth as a sphere: "It is He who sits above the *circle* of the earth" (Isaiah 40:22) and, "He hangs the earth on nothing" (Job 26:7). The Koran insisted earth was flat: "Do they not consider . . . How the earth has been flattened out?" (Koran 88:20). And, "the earth We have spread out." (Koran 15.19).

4a. Arabs believed in Jinn (Genies), (Jinni for single): a Jahiliya legend inspired by the infinite deserts and ghostly mountains of Hijaz and Yemen. A jinni is a spirit capable of assuming human or animal form and exercising supernatural influence over man. The Koran came to reassert their existence: "We created man from mud and gravel and created Jinn from a fiery fusion," (Koran). Their interaction with mankind is unquestionable: "true, there were persons among mankind who took shelter with *persons* among the Jinn, but they increased their folly." (Koran 72:6).

On a Friday Q & A T.V. program a caller informed the cleric that he was in love with a Jinni girl and asked his

'Fatwa' for the possibility of marrying her. The cleric answered without hesitation: 'Yes, if the wedding is concluded according to the Sinna of Allah and his Prophet?!' Muhammad himself advocated Jinn's omnipotence: "every one of you is escorted by a jinni and an angel," he once preached his followers. "Even you, messenger of Allah?" someone asked. "Even me," Muhammad answered, "but Allah helped me and *he was converted to Islam*, since that time he does order me to do good." (Ibn Hisham). A Muslim thinker ponders today: what kind of suggestions did the jinni give the Prophet before turning to Islam? And how could Jinn become Muslim? Allah is more knowledgeable!

The Koran declares that the jinn are evil creatures associated with Satan: "Satan was one of the jinn and he broke the command of his lord." (Koran 18:50). The jinn occupy one whole chapter of the Koran called "Surat Al-Jinn." In that chapter the jinn told Muhammad, "Amongst us are some who are Muslims (literal)." (Koran 72:14) The rest of the Sura recorded words of the jinn as "revealed words" in line with the Koranic style. An Arab poet is believed to have his own Jinni that inspires him the subject as well as the suitable rhythm.

4.b. Christian Khadija who did not believe in Jinn apparently mocked—or teased Muhammad when he came to her one day shivering from 'a spirit that touched him.' Ibn Hisham, the trusted biographer of the Prophet has the story: "Khadija asked: 'would you please tell me when the spirit comes to you?' When Muhammad told her of the spirit's arrival she said: 'Muhammad, sit on my left thigh.' Muhammad did. 'Do you see the spirit?' she asked. 'Yes'. 'Then sit on my right thigh.' He did. 'Do you see the spirit?' she asked. 'Yes' he answered. 'Then sit on my lap.' He did. 'Do you see the spirit?' 'Yes' he answered. Then Khadija uncovered a *feminine part* of her body while Muhammad was on her lap. 'Do you see the spirit *now*?' 'No' he answered. Then Khadija said: 'Muhammad, that spirit was an angel not a devil.'(Ibn Hisham-Part 2—74/75). A strange way indeed to identify a spirit!

According to Jahiliyia—as well as Islamic belief Jinn are half-human and half-demon creatures. They were originally spirits by nature that went around causing madness and poetic inspiration in humans. Like humans they reproduce, have the same basic bodily needs and they can die as well even though their life span is much longer than humans'. It is also believed that a few of the jinn serve Allah. Arabs believed jinn usually took the form of ostriches or even rode them. There are five different class orders of genies. The Marid is the most powerful, the Afrit, the Shaitan, the Jinn, and finally the Jann which is the least powerful. The Jinn are believed to do good or evil. But they are mischievous and cunning. They enjoy punishing humans for the wrongs done to them even accidentally. Thus accidents and diseases done to humans are considered to be of their making. They can assume both physical animal or human forms. They can exist in the air, in flame, beneath the earth and in inanimate objects like the legendary Aladin Lamp!

Besides Jinn and their constant interfacing with people many other Jahiliya practices and beliefs were adopted by Islam to provide an effortless conversion; few among them: the yearly pilgrimage to Mecca and its ritual of strolling around the Qaaba, the lunar months and their names updated later by Omar, marrying more than one woman at the same time, the Jahiliya's absolute backing among clanship that became after Islam: "support your brother Muslim whether oppressor or oppressed"; and much more . . .

Like the Hebrew scripture that was challenged lately by the controversial Qumran scrolls the Koran had its own challenge by a similar 'find' in Yemen. In 1972 during the restoration of the Great Mosque of Sana'a, laborers working in a loft between the structure's inner and outer roofs stumbled across a remarkable gravesite and unearthed a mash of old parchment and paper documents tempered by centuries of dampness. The laborers gathered up the manuscripts, pressed them into some twenty sacks and set them aside. Judge Esmail al-Akwa' of the Yemeni Antiquities Authority realized the importance of the find and sought German assistance in examining and preserving the fragments.

In 1981 Gerd-R. Puin, a specialist in Koranic paleography based at Saarland University, Germany was sent to organize and oversee the restoration project. His preliminary inspection revealed unconventional verse orderings, minor textual variations and rare styles of orthography in early Hijazi Arabic script and artistic embellishment. The sheets seemed to suggest an *evolving* text rather than simple revelation early in that same century.

Muslims would rush to attack any meddling in this sort of thinking. Yet the Koran may prove to be a scripture with a history like any other except that such history has been suppressed to any investigation. Studying it would provoke howls of protest especially when such studies are performed in the West whose apparent aim is to tamper with the Muslim legacy at a time when Muslims are not trying to destroy anyone's faith.

FOURTEEN

Koran/Bible Connections

"We have made it a Koran in Arabic; that you may be able to understand. It is in the 'Mother of the Book' with us, high and full of wisdom".

Koran 43-3/4

The fact that the Koran is basically an Arabic reading of the Ebionite Mathew's Gospel according to the Hebrews is obvious throughout the original Meccan verses that were later dispersed by Othman. It is a "detailed" (conveyed translation) of the original Mother of Books. It insists on the Kitabis to believe in as it was an authenticated rendering of their scripture: "O you people of the Book, believe in what we have revealed, confirming what is with you" (Koran 4-47). That scripture,—the Koran further explains—was always the origin of what is revealed: "It is not a tale invented, but a confirmation of what is in his hands, and a guide and mercy to those who believe" (Koran 13-111).

Therefore we find between the Arabian Koran and the Hebrew/Aramaic Gospel a great and frequent textual resemblance. We list hereunder various examples on the most important subjects in Koranic verses followed in *italics* by their corresponding Gospel origins:

1- The Virgin Mary:

Salutation this could be. And the angel said unto her, fear not Mary, for you have found favor with God. (The Gospels)

"He said: so it will be, your Lord says: "that is easy for me; and (We wish) to appoint him as a sign unto men and a mercy from Us; it is a decreed matter" (Koran 19:21).

"And the childbirth pains drove her to the trunk of a palm tree; she cried: "Ah, would that I had died before this and be forgotten and out of sight" . . . "A voice cried to her from beneath the tree: "give not, for the lord has provided a rivulet beneath you" . . . "And shake towards you the trunk of the palm tree; it will let fall fresh ripe dates upon you" (Koran 19:23.25).

Then said Mary unto the angel, how shall this be seeing I know not a man?

He said behold, you shall conceive in your womb and bring fourth a son and shall call his name Jesus. He shall be great and shall be called the Son of the Highest . . .

And the angel answered and said unto her, the Holy Ghost shall come upon you and the power of the highest shall overshadow you; therefore also that holy thing which shall be born of you shall be called the Son of God. (Jacob and Mathew)

The story of Hagar in Genesis, where Hagar was lost in wilderness with no water and "she cast the child under one of the shrubs", "she sat over against him and lift up her voice and wept . . . but God said unto her: "what ails you Hagar, for God has heard the voice of the lad . . . arise and lift him up. And God opened her eyes and she saw a well of water . . ." (Genesis21:14.21).

2- On Alms and Charities:

"Those who spend their substance in the cause of God and follow not their gifts with reminders of their generosity or with injury, for them their reward is with their Lord . . . O you who believe, cancel not your charities by reminders or injury, like those who spend their substance to be seen of men . . ." (Koran 2: 262-264).

"When you do your alms do not sound a trumpet before you, as the hypocrites do in the synagogues and in the streets, that they may have glory of men . . . You do not your alms before men to be seen of them; otherwise you have no reward of your Father who is in heavens" (Mat. 6:2-1).

"We will not fail to reward those who do good." (Koran 12:56).

"He that does good shall have ten times as much to his credit." (Koran 6:160)

"Those who loan God a good loan shall be rewarded many folds and be given a good credit." (Koran 57:18).

"He who will give . . . a cup of cold water . . . shall in no wise lose his reward." (Matthew 10:42)

"Jesus to Peter: Everyone that has forsaken houses, brothers or sisters, or father or mother . . . for my name's sake, shall receive a hundredfold . . ." (Mat.19:29)

3- On the Last Day:

"The angels descend on the people" . . . "Find them" . . . "And meet them" . . . "And enter upon them from every door" . . . "And God comes to them in canopies of clouds and angels." (Koran 2:210 and various).

"Behold, the Lord comes with ten thousands of his saints, to execute judgment upon all, and to convince all that are ungodly among them of all their bad deeds . . ." (Jude 14-15).

"And angels gather by columns" . . . "And there will be lightening and thunders and great terrors" . . . "And there will be great hunger." (Koran 24:43 and various).

"God sends his angels by the trumpet" . . . "And there will be famine in various places" (Mat. 24:7).

"When the trumpet is sounded" . . . "A mighty blast is heard all over under which the Earth tremble, and mighty men shudder" (Koran: various).

"And the trumpet is sounded" . . . *"And a great sound of blast is heard all over under which all nations of the earth will tremble"* (Mat. 24:30).

"The day you shall see, when every nursing mother shall forget her suckling-babe, and every pregnant female shall drop her load. You shall see mankind as in a drunken riot, yet not drunk: but dreadful will be the wrath of God." (Koran 22:2).

"And woes unto them that are with child and to them that give suck in those days" . . . *"And shall be great tribulation such as was not since the beginning of the world to this time, no, nor ever shall be."* (Mat. 24:19-21).

"It renders the young old" . . . "That day shall a man flee from his own brother . . . and his mother and father . . . and his wife and children . . . each one of them in that day, will have enough concern to make him indifferent to the others."(Koran 80: 34)

"In it a brother delivers his brother to death and children will kill their parents" . . .

"Nobody would intercede to anybody: not a father, a mother, a friend or a relative. Nobody will replace anybody. Each is with his own concern" (Mat. & various).

"On that day, no wealth or children will be useful" . . . And those who bragged: "We have more in wealth and sons and we cannot be punished." (Koran 34:36).

"Their silver and their gold shall not be able to deliver them in the day of wrath of the Lord . . ." (Ezekiel 8:19).

In it, people are steered before God "separated apart" . . . the favored will be "those on the right" . . . "And the wrongdoers in the left" . . . "On the day when their tongues, their hands and their feet will bear witness against them for their actions." (Koran 24:24).

"And before him shall be gathered all nations; and he shall separate them one from another, as a shepherd divides his sheep from the goats. And he shall set the sheep on his right hands but the goats on the left . . ." (Mat. 25:32-33).

Above samples of similitude are very common throughout the Koranic texts. They confirm two distinct aspects: 1/ the unquestioned relationship between the Meccan Koran and the Aramaic Gospel and 2/ the metaphorical—conveyed—translation that was in fact what is best described by the Arabian Koran itself: "detailing," "replication," "easiness" and "admonition." Far from the literal translation we know today.

FIFTEEN

Arab Women in Jahiliya

"I verily stand fitting for distinguished living
I walk with dignity, am pretty and charming
My cheek is offered to my lover's kiss
And with my embrace, a joy he won't miss."

A Bedouin poetess

Arab women from Jahiliya through Islam until our modern times were always in a downhill degeneration course. It is important to trace what Arab and Muslim women have suffered through ages and the drastic changes that led to their stature today. Those changes motivated many

151

Western as well as Muslim thinkers to retraces glimpses into that pre-Islamic era and women's conditions in it.

Islam divides Jahiliya in two eras. The early 'first one', where women enjoyed full freedom to the point of displaying an extravagant maquillage with Henna and all available cosmetics, having free sex and asking the hands of men in marriage; these were the times of Queen Sheba and her flourishing Saba'a province around the Mareb Dam that became later the Tagleb tribe area. The Prophet mentioned this first period when he scorned his wives: "and don't adorn yourselves the adornment of the First Jahiliya . . ." The Second Jahiliya probably started before the Roman conquest of the Levant where Arabia lacked a good ruler and went through endless tribal feuds. Women then missed their cosmopolitan finesse and experienced tough and secluded Bedouin life where the Sheik of the tribe is the ruler. The tribe was the main unit of the society. Each consisted of a group of kindred clans; every clan was made up of members of "Hayy" or encampment; each tent sheltered a family. The bond of blood connected together all members of the same tribe who submitted to the authority of the Sheik. A Sheik is usually selected by the clan elders from one of the prominent families to act as an arbitrator over internal conflicts. The fact that certain clans prefixed their names with feminine names is an indication of an ancient matriarchal culture that existed in Arabia long before Islam. Blood solidarity ("asabiyah") was the spirit of the tribe: an unconditional loyalty to fellow tribesmen.

The tribe regarded every other tribe as an enemy unless they had forged alliances to protect one another. In order to survive every individual had to be affiliated with a tribe. Warfare was the means of settling disputes and maintaining order. That is why Arabs who associated later with Islam used the same style tribal raids basically for the same purposes on other recalcitrant tribes to bring them into submission. Only this time the Sheik was Muhammad, the Prophet of Allah and the Caliphs after him; the "asabiyah' turned to solidarity in Islam.

Laws and customs in this tribal society varied from one area to another. For this reason, we find different accounts of women's status but general indications that women held high social positions and exerted great influence. They freely chose their husbands, had the right to divorce and could return to their own people if they were unhappy or mistreated. They were regarded as equals, not as slaves and were the inspiration of many poets and warriors being the only beautiful "things" in the dreary desert. An example of a brave woman from this era is Fukayha who protected a man seeking refuge in her tent while being pursued by the enemy. She courageously covered him with her smock and with her sword drawn prevented his pursuers from capturing him until her brothers came to his defense thereby saving his life. Bedouin girls were as strong willed and aggressive as their male counterparts. Many among them were horsewomen who carried weapons and participated in fights. Many had the gift of poetry which they often chanted to lament the dead. Most of them would use poetry to hearten warriors and raise their spirits:

"We, the pretty girls of Tareq*, have no fear.
Walk on silken sheets embroidered in Oufir**
We'll dump you if defeated with no tears shed
But hug you if winners and take you to bed . . ."

*Tribe's name ** Indian town at the mouth of Indus river.

153

A hero's mother and sisters were deemed most worthy of mourning and praising him; a proof of the high character and position of women in pre-Islamic Arabia.

Literally, Jahiliya means ignorance. This is still how it is wrongly understood and generalized: the Age of Darkness. The real meanings though were far different: it is the state of being an independent lone eagle and that hard-nosed attitude of aloofness. Jahilyia did in no way mean lack of knowledge but simply self-induced unawareness and feigning indifference; an ancient 'not-giving-a-damn' attitude illustrated by poet Amr Bin Kolthum:

"Let nobody feign indifference over us as we promise;
We shall feign indifference much above his."

Describing a tribal raid unto his encampment the poet said:

"When I saw our girls scurrying over the arid land
And saw Lamees * as a bright moon overland
Her hidden beauty unveiled: a serious matter indeed . . .
I fought their hero to death, my duty and my creed:
They bet on my blood: an' I bet to swordfight
Many are those entombed under my hands, and sight:
All the good men I knew have gone far away . . .
Am left alone like a sword; that is how I will stay."

(*) A girl's name meaning 'soft at touch.'

Even poetic translation does not carry the powerful emotions of love, bravery, sorrow and arrogance of the poet.

This short poem depicts the plight of the Bedouin where love and hatred, life and death are daily occurrences. Almost all Jahiliya poems and much of the Islamic ones started with a short or long female beauty description. That was the starting appetizer for people to memorize; exactly like cover-girls on our magazines today. Women in Arabia were more than sources of love and beauty but of maddening infatuation. Poets went to their best superlatives to describe their attractiveness and heart-felt passionate torment with them.

This individualist attitude stimulated the Bedouin to excel and outclass others in a line all his own: poetry. His rich Arabic language gave him abundant figures of speech to attain the most intricate nuances and capture nearly all evading human thoughts or natural features. Orientalists have been amazed at the profundity and emotional intensity of Arabian poets; a good number among them were females with Khansaa in the forefront. The Jahiliya poetry inheritance remains today a most cherished Arabian legacy.

Curiously enough, an Arabian poem was inspired by the Bedouin encampment itself: each verse is a "Beit" or tent, composed of a "Sadr", the front part of the verse—or the tent compartment where men sit, and the "Ajoz", the back part where old women "Ajooz" sit. The number of "Beits" in the single poem, their emotions and expressiveness, determine the talent and rank of the poet comparable in extent to the dimension of the tribe's encampment itself.

The lonesome attitude inherent to the Bedouin as to his camel or horse made him dig in unabashed through the many adversities and hardships of his desert life to emerge victorious or meet his bust. To confront calamities and repel raids his best bet was to maximize his male children and minimize females. Females were a problem to defend in raids and a risk of becoming hostages; a big blow to honor and prestige.

Hence the infanticide (Wa'ad) of females was common practice. The Koran admonishes the Arabs against killing their children for fear of poverty and promises sustenance for them: "do not kill your children for fear of poverty: it is We who shall provide sustenance for them as well as for you. Verily, killing them is a great sin." (Koran 17:31) The reason for that custom was not only the fear of poverty but the avoidance of young women captivities and related predicaments; a known fact yet a taboo to talk about. Female infanticide however should not be the sole basis for assessing the status of women. Because of that hideous habit that status was further enhanced in a predominantly male society. Arabia was a diverse tribal network where women's rights varied according to the prevailing customs and traditions. To claim that Arab women were universally inferior to men and had absolutely no rights before Islam is grossly biased.

Polygamy was also a common tradition. While in Islam a man can marry up to four; within some tribes a single woman may sleep with several males until she is declared pregnant by one of them; only then she becomes his wife. Bedouins' craving to sire only males was so intense that they would avoid copulation with any of their women who delivered two girls in a raw, much to the distress of this woman poetess who had that problem:

"Why Abu Noman doesn't approach us.
He keeps dwelling in the tent next to us.
Infuriated: we don't deliver him a male.
By Allah, who could accept that tale?
We gave him what he had given us!"

The number of women a man could marry depended on his rank, sexual potential and spending power. Besides the declared wives from whom male children were produced, whatever 'his right hand' could garner is also his. Concubines, many of them from Abyssinia and East Africa competed favorably with Arab girls. They may not be freed but their male infants could gain parenthood later if they prove worthy. This Jahiliya practice was duplicated by Islam with no major changes.

Pre-Islamic Arabia was under the rule of Persia then Constantinople with little attention given to this arid and meaningless land. Only big towns like Medina, Mecca, Najran and Aden were significant thanks to the caravan trade routes. Some relations among Byzantine and Christian tribes were established along with commercial ties between Damascus, the Byzantine southern capital, and the Arab trading moguls. Soon enough those cities acquired their cosmopolitan characteristics where countless Arab women like Khadija, started to relinquish the rough Bedouin habits and indulge in the dolce vita styles of those days; chief among them was Mecca. Lesbian practices flourishes among women: the famous and pretty wife of king Noman bin Munzer was openly in love with a Yemeni girlfriend, Haisa. Her husband was in the know and tolerated it!

157

We can picture the looks of a typical Meccan woman from the many descriptions in poetry as well as the Koran. Her headwear consisted of a long scarf (Khimar) ornamented with silver—or gold chain on top of the front allowing her hair to appear on both sides of her face. The scarf could be turned at will to cover the neck or lower part of the face to avoid cold or sand, hinder intrusive eyes—or attract them. The top wear was an embroidered, half-sleeve jacket reaching the lower waist with large open lapels (Joyoub) in front allowing a substantial bosom view. From the waist down come long and fluffy pantalets (Sarwal) over short underwear or a long skirt (Thob). The jewelry outfit is the same as today plus the "Domloj": a couple of thick foot bangles worn over the ankles to produce attracting jingling while walking. The footwear consisted of various low-heel sandals. An embroidered, long cloak may be turned over the shoulders in cool weather. The veil of Muslim women today was then inexistent.

Because of the emphasis on the tribe and the variation of customs, marriage was a flexible institution with no strict rules. Based on the literary sources it is likely that the following forms of marriage existed in pre-Islamic Arabia at one time or another:

- The **marriage by agreement** was concluded with consent between the man and the woman's family. If the husband was from another tribe the woman often left her family and found a permanent home in her husband's tribe. The tribe which received the woman kept her children unless there was a special contract to restore the offspring of the marriage to the mother's people.

- The **marriage by capture** was a universal practice before and after Islam. In times of war women were often captured and taken to the slave market of a trading place such as Mecca and sold into marriage or slavery. Slave markets remained until last century when King Faisal abolished them in Saudi Arabia. In this kind of marriage classified as a "marriage of dominion," the husband was called the woman's lord or owner (Baal), not just in Arabia but also among the Hebrews and Canaanites.

- The **marriage by purchase** where the woman's family gave her away for a price called the dowry ("mahr"), which usually consisted of camels and horses and liquid money in our days.

- The **marriage by inheritance** was a widespread custom throughout Arabia including Medina and Mecca whereby the heir of the deceased inherited his wife. He could then keep her as a wife or give her away in marriage for a dowry.

- The **temporary ("Mot'a") pleasure marriage** was—and still is—a purely personal contract founded on consent between a man and a woman without any intervention on the part of the woman's family or need for witnesses. In this type of marriage the woman does not leave her home, her people give up no rights which they had over her and the children of such marriage do not belong to the husband nor are they entitled to an inheritance.

There were other types of marriage or cohabitation such as **secret cohabitation** which has been frequently described in

Arabic poetry. In this case the woman only received occasional visits from the man she loved. The man often belonging to a hostile tribe visits his beloved in secret. Although the poets usually described them as forbidden love affairs the relations were usually well-known and no cause to shame or punishment; the secrecy was simply a matter of etiquette. There are also indications that **polyandry** (marrying more than one husband) existed which had its roots in an ancient, defunct matriarchal culture. **Wife-lending** was a practice whereby husbands allowed their wives to live with "men of distinction" to produce noble offspring. Having concubines was more economical and another reason to avoid costly polygamy.

Women of Mecca were in a relatively better position than those of Medina although marriages by capture and purchase were also practiced in Mecca. Bedouin women on the other hand enjoyed more freedom and asserted themselves more strongly than women of the sedentary tribes. The reason for this was perhaps due to the conditions of nomad life which made the strict seclusion of women impossible, so it allowed a further development of an independent female character. Although the Bedouin woman lived in a polygamous family under a marriage of dominion, she could freely choose a husband and leave him at will. With only small variations most of the above marriage fashions are in Islam to this day governed by Koranic resolutions.

SIXTEEN

The Waning Woman in Islam

"Clerics differ with me over what times we are living in. It is not democracy when a man can talk about politics without anyone threatening him. Democracy is when a woman can talk of her lover without anybody killing her".

Dr. Souad Al-Sabah—Kuwait University

The advent of Islam shifted the focus from the tribe to the individual balanced by the concept of community and family but failed to institute a system in which everyone was equal regardless of his/her gender, race, age or wealth. Tribal affiliations were subdued but women's rights diminished in the later part of Muhammad's life. Islam reduced women's rights as a free human being by harnessing her responsibilities and obligations. Thus she became more restricted under Islam as opposed to Jahiliya. Even in those tribes that had been most oppressive to women Islam did not improve women's conditions, dignity and status but rather downgraded those to lower echelons.

The personal lifestyle of the Prophet and his companions was the dominating criteria that affected women's future life. Muhammad for instance loathed those chest lapels 'Joyoub' opening and asked his wives through the Koran to tighten them as deemed attractive to other men, especially after he received remarks from poignant Omar that many men were in touch with them during his absence. He was also realizing that among this large Harem he was but a single, aged man unable to satisfy each of them to the point that the elders among them willingly ceded their 'night' to the younger. So a revelation came to him ordering his wives as well as other Muslim women to seek decency: "O Prophet! Advise your wives and daughters, and the believing women, that they should cast their outer lapels over their chests (when out of home): that is most convenient, that they should be known [as such] and not molested. And Allah is oft-forgiving, most merciful." (Koran 33:59). When his wives asked his permission to adorn themselves like other women and wanted him to raise their allowance the answer came negative: "O Prophet! Say to your consorts: if it be that you desire the life of this world and its glitter—then come! I will provide for your enjoyment and set you free in a handsome manner." (Koran 33:28). Translation: he would give them money and divorce them. The sword of divorce was always ready to threaten Muhammad's wives and subdue them in the name of Allah. The same sword remains today in men's hands.

Further dire changes actually occurred during the later part of Muhammad's life and the major depressing ones precisely on the evening he married Zeinab bint Jahsh. To understand the various negative measures against women, a review of Muhammad's personal life is important.

The would-be Prophet had a confused and deprived childhood as we had seen. His teen and manhood years unfolded in a poverty stricken home where any sexual experience was not within reach. The Mecca pleasure houses frequented by his rich peers were closed to him. His long caravan trips to Damascus and Yemen unveiled many delights but did little to quench his sexual thirst. If we add to that his constant alienation and the recurring convulsions he would go through intermittently (as expressed by Abu Taleb) we can conclude that Muhammad had a very miserable personal life at the time his manhood was swelling.

Marrying at 25 a woman the age of his mother gave him fresh sexual problems. The twice-widowed matriarch of several children granted Muhammad lots of motherly love, affection, smooth life and financial security but no sexual gratification. The young man must have remembered his mother Amina and probably saw her in Khadija. Muhammad was bound by his Nazarene marriage to live with Khadija through her next twenty years until her death, all the while suppressing his desert masculinity.

When the lady of dignity and opulence passed away he unleashed his sexual desires and in a span of ten years married twelve wives in addition to his many concubines. Not one of them was mentioned in the Koran by name; in fact the only woman's name in the Koran was Mary. On his victorious conquest of Mecca he ordered the idols and icons of the Kaaba destroyed, all except one that he covered with his hands: the icon of Mary and baby Jesus. Islam developed disregard to women and considered anything related to them degrading and humiliating. The late Emir of Eastern Saudi Arabia, Bin Jalawi, wanted once to give his son the extreme punishment for an offense he committed: he imprisoned the young lad for one month in the Harem apartments! A foreigner was once invited to a wedding in a large house with two entrances for males and females, he headed to the wrong door when an usher rushed to take his hand and redirect him saying: 'this way, 'azzak Allah' (may Allah lift you from—that—low).

Polygamy was unleashed in the Koran: "marry such women as seem good to you, two, three, and four; but if you fear you will not be equitable, then only one, or what your right hands own; so it is likelier you will not be partial". (Koran 4:3). In defending polygamy, Ayatollah Gomi of Iran told Parisian LE MONDE, January 20, 1979: "most Europeans have mistresses. Why should we suppress human instincts? A rooster satisfies several hens and a stallion several mares. A woman is unavailable during certain periods where a man is always active and ready." In the Islamic slave trade mostly from East Africa two females would be priced for one male. Very large numbers of slaves were used for domestic purposes. Concubine collection was a prestige for those who could afford and there was no disrepute attached to having women as sexual objects. Some enormous harems could be a status symbol comparable to collecting cars by people today.

To further understand why Muslims in modern times still marry as much as four women in addition to "whatever your right hand can garner" we have to revert to the Koran: "You have indeed in the Messenger of Allah an excellent paradigm." (Koran 33:21). Muslims therefore believe it right to follow the Prophet's example—although he was singled out among the believers—and rally as much women as their physical and financial capabilities permit. Four women were not enough to Muhammad; the revelation to marry any number of women he wished came as follows: "O Prophet! We have made lawful to you your wives to whom you had paid their dowers; and those whom your right hand possesses out of the captives of war whom Allah has assigned to you; and daughters of your paternal uncles and aunts, and daughters of your maternal uncles and aunts who migrated with you; and any believing woman who gives herself to the Prophet if the Prophet wishes to wed her—this only for you, and not for the believers [at large]; we know what we have appointed for them as to their wives and the captives whom their right hands possess—in order that there should be no difficulty for you. And Allah is oft forgiving, most merciful." (Koran 33:50).

Dr. Seymour Gray of Brooklyn, Mass. author of "Beyond the Veil—The Adventures of an American Doctor in Saudi Arabia" in charge of the King Faisal Specialist Hospital in

Riyadh 1975-78 was asked if he really believed the late King Ibn Saud, founder of modern Saudi Arabia had married 300 women in his lifetime. He said "I don't know if Ibn Saud was married to precisely 300 women, but that approximate number, give or take a dozen or two, seems to be correct."

Muslim clerics defend Allah's lavish appropriation to Muhammad as he had moral responsibilities and political accountability towards those distressed women widowed in wars (actually, only three wives were under this duress). These same clerics are unheard of when it comes to wealthy modern Muslims and the count of how many women—and concubines—'their right hands' could pile up. The big controversy in any Muslim woman's life is that when she commits adultery she is stoned to death while her husband may roam the East and the West collecting concubines!

Islam however made it difficult if not impossible to prove adultery: It necessitates four different witnesses to testify under oath having seen the actual *act of penetration*! Anyone accusing or testifying otherwise is subject to punishment. Caliph Omar acquitted Ibn Shuba who committed adultery with a woman named Omm Jameel. He hinted to Zyad Ibn Samila, one of the four witnesses to bear out in support of Ibn Shuba. Zyad testified against three other eye witnesses who confirmed they saw Ibn Shuba in the act. Caliph Omar accepted the testimony of Zyad, acquitted Ibn Shuba and ordered him to beat the three eyewitnesses who testified against him (The Legend and Heritage, page 266). Hence the Muslim society that appears openly as the most pious and conservative nation on earth is in fact awash with sexual extravaganza including incest, gays and lesbians all under cover and behind locked doors. Historical examples:

1. To escape the rigorous regimen of their Caliphate in Damascus and enjoy some dolce vita, the Umayyad Caliphs established at Anjar, Lebanon, a palatial fun city built with scavenged remnants of Phoenician and Roman temples scattered in the Bekaa valley. The secluded and well guarded town was full of war-prize concubines from all over the ancient world, furnished with the plushest appointments Damascus could offer and filled with the best foods, fruits and wines of Lebanon. Their thousand-and-one-night retreat in Anjar surpassed in opulence—and orgies—any known Roman outpost. The ruins of Anjar remain today a historic and tourist site on all tours itineraries.

2. Under Haroun Alrashid and his Abbasid successors, homosexuality was the fashion of the day. Dignitaries openly owned their male lovers the way people own cell phones today. Poet abu Nowas mentioned his male lovers many times. Caliph Alwasic was himself homosexual. His partner was an attractive young man called Muhag. It is said: If Muhag gets angry with Alwasic and refuses to have sex with him the Caliph would suspend all government activities until Muhag resumes his relationship (The Hidden Truth. 124). Alwasic was the last Caliph in the Abbasid dynasty.

3. While Homosexuality is basically against Islamic belief to the point that Haroun Alrashid beheaded a couple of "Sahaqia", lesbians caught in the act in his palace, it

is much in fashion today among males and females in the Muslim world than in the West but generally taboo and disguised. In Dubai and the rest of the Gulf gays are called "Saroukh"—rockets and are conspicuous among the wealthy traders and government officials living the good life by skimming off the systems. Some 'marriages' among them are made public.

The Prophet gave his followers some golden rules: "if you are plagued with sins, cover up so you may make it". And: "treat your wanton needs with concealment". These rules were apparently followed and proved disastrous to the Muslim mind: by concealing shortcomings and wrongdoings Muslims are automatically distanced from realism, honesty and openness.

The recorded list of Muhammad's wives *after* Khadija is:

- Suda, daughter of Zamma.
- Aisha daughter of Abu Bakr
- Hafsa, daughter of Omar.
- Zainab, daughter of Khuzima.
- Om Sulma, her name was Hind.
- Jewariah, daughter of Al-Harith.
- Zainab daughter of Jahsh
- Safia, daughter of Huyay, a Jewess whose husband was killed with many Jews during the Khyber siege. She was seventeen years old and very beautiful.
- Om Habiba.

There are five other wives, who are not mentioned by Ibn Hisham,

- Sharaaf, daughter of Khalifa.
- Al-Alia, daughter of Zabian.
- Wasna, daughter of Al-Naaman.
- Maria, the Egyptian Coptic Christian who was given to Muhammad by Al-Mokawkas, the ruler of Coptic Egypt. She bore Muhammad's only son Ibrahim who died when he was two years old. She did not convert to Islam.
- Maimona, daughter of Harith.

Plus many concubines and hostages acquired as gifts or through various raids.

Two of these women, **Aisha bint Abu Bakr** and **Zainab bint Jahsh** left major imprints on the fate of Muslim women. We will study them with some details:

After marrying another widowed woman, Suda, whose husband migrated to Abyssinia and died there, Muhammad yearned for a virgin to confirm and restore his desert virility. Aisha, daughter of Abu Bakr, the attractive, talkative, voluble and spontaneous petite met all specifications. He used to visit his best friend's house just to see her. The six year old would sit on his knees and temper with his beard. Baby Aisha revived the prophet's early teens and his crave to a female known but to him. Her pure, coquettish face would haunt his imagination. He decided after careful deliberations to get Aisha and free himself of his many sexual obstructions.

"Muhammad married her when he was fifty three years old and she was only six years old. He had to wait three years until she started her menses and had intercourse with her when she was nine years old." (The Wives of the Prophet, 57-61). This 'example' of a child abuse was copied by his other companions: Omar, much older than Ali, would marry his baby daughter and would propose his young but not so pretty girl Hafsa to his senior Abu Bakr. The Consultative House junta is in charge: they chart and execute whatever pleases them! When Muhammad married Aisha he set an example to all Muslims.

The following story was sent recently by a mother to a renowned Egyptian magazine: "My problem is . . . my husband came home with a friend who is about his age. He requested that our daughter "Marwa" who is nine years old bring tea to his friend. At night he told me with great joy that his fifty years old friend agreed to marry "Marwa." When I objected he told me that he is following Prophet Muhammad's example who engaged Aisha when she was six years old and had sex with her when she was nine years old as is written in Sahih Al-Bukhary."

To this day older Muslim men marry minor girls following that example. Such countless child abuses take place across the Muslim world using this religious umbrella. If we consider that many of these crimes are done by men who are already married who would add wives to their household probably younger than their children, one can imagine the tremendous discords and unruliness Muslim families are wallowing in.

Aisha was a live wire in her dealings with Muhammad; her childish, outspoken cynicism was perceptible when it comes to relationship and even revelations. One day she complained to him of a headache, he nonchalantly answered by a similar complaint of his, she told him: "I think you want me to die and if that should happen you would spend the rest of the day sleeping with one of your wives!". In one of his convulsions he told her: "Aisha, it is Gabriel, he says hello to you . . ." she told him: "oh yes, give him my regards . . ." (Sahih Bukhari).

Aisha, the youngest who reached her 16 when the Prophet died wanted to remain the most cherished in the harem. She was very jealous of fresh brides, especially the Egyptian Coptic blonde slave, curly-haired Maria whose son and heir Ibrahim died at two allegedly through a conspiracy orchestrated by Aisha and Hafsa. She was also jealous of the aristocratic Zainab bint Jahsh. She once asked him, "How come women offer themselves to you?" The revelation immediately descended: "you may defer any of them you wish and take to yourself any you wish, and if you desire any you have set aside no sin is chargeable to you." [Koran 33:51]. She exclaimed: "It seems to me that your Lord hastens to satisfy your desire." (Bukhary).

Aisha conspired again with his other wives when he had a quickie with Maria in the bed of his wife Hafsa, daughter of Omar. Muhammad became angry of them all and refused to share their beds. Actually he made himself a tent on the roof that he would climb to on a ladder and deserted them for one whole month. Ali knew of her conspiracy and counseled the Prophet in his own way: "Prophet of Allah, Arab women are all at your disposal, why don't you divorce them all and get fresh consorts better than them?" This advice reached Aisha and made her steam. Ali added insult to injury and

openly advised him to divorce Aisha when she was accused
of adultery. All that cropped up to create a died-in-the-wool
enmity between her and Ali. She was instrumental in
distancing him from the Caliphate upon Muhammad's
death and later fought him at the head of an army that she
personally led from her camel's howdah. Though the famous
"Battle of the Camel" was easily won by Ali, it was a great
political embarrassment to him fighting a woman's army.
Moawia in Damascus enjoyed the scene very much.

Aisha was constantly burning for undelivered sex and
green of jealousy to say the least. She was always conspiring
with her clan of women against those pretty newcomers.
A case in point is when Muhammad married Christian
Asma, daughter of Al-Noman, a very attractive young lady
indeed. "Aisha conspired with Hafsa and others to abort
this marriage. They went to Asma and advised her that the
Prophet is a deeply religious man who likes words of Allah.
They asked her to say to Muhammad when he comes in to
her "I seek refuge in Allah from you" if she wanted to please
him. The novice bride in Islamic phraseology believed them.
When Muhammad came into her room she said "I seek
refuge in Allah from you." Hearing that he said: "you picked
the ultimate refuge", and sent her back to her parents." (Ibn
Hisham). Aisha marked one meager point.

Muhammad could not afford to heed Ali's advice and
divorce his wives; his primary ones were daughters of his
leading companions. Instead, he received the following
revelation: "When the Prophet disclosed a matter in
confidence to one of his consorts, and she then divulged it
[to another], and Allah made it known to him, he confirmed

part thereof and passed over a part. Then when he told her thereof, she said, "Who told you this?" He said, "He told me Who is the Knower, the Aware." If you two (Aisha and Hafsa) turn in repentance to Allah, your hearts are indeed so inclined; but if you back up each other against him, truly Allah is his Protector, and so Gabriel, and every righteous one among those who believe and furthermore, the angels will back (him) up. It may be, if he divorced you all, that Allah will give him in exchange consorts better than you (Ali's hint)—who submit their wills, who believe, who are devout; who turn to Allah in repentance, who worship in humility, who fast—previously married or *virgins*." (Koran 66:3-5).

The word '*virgins*' is meant for Aisha. She was bragging to have been the only virgin Muhammad married!? In an effort to lure him more to her she once alluded to him: "suppose you landed in a valley where there were trees of which something had been eaten and then found a tree of which nothing had been eaten, on which tree would you let your camel graze?"—he said that he would let his camel graze on the tree of which nothing had been eaten." (Bukhari).

Muhammad's wives were scared. They repented. The revelation did what he wanted and he came back down from his tent to them. Yet he was troubled some of them might commit lewdness behind his back especially those young ones; the following revelation came to threaten them and instill terror in their hearts: "O you, wives of the Prophet. Whosoever of you commits manifest lewdness, the punishment for her will be doubled, and that is easy for Allah (Koran 33:30). This same bombardment comes today on the heads of Muslim women through either the clerics in mosques and on

TV's or by their husbands. As to men they enjoy full freedom with whatever their right hands possess.

Aisha's alleged adultery story dubbed the (Ifk) or 'fib' incident is best narrated by herself: "It was decided that I should accompany him during the raid on Banu Mustaliq. On the return journey we halted for the night before resuming to Medina. It was still night when they began to make preparations for the march. So I went outside the camp to ease myself. When I returned and came near my halting place I noticed that my necklace had fallen down somewhere. I went back in search for it but in the meantime the caravan moved off and I was left behind all alone. They must have thought I was in my howdah when they departed. I stayed waiting for an expedition to pick me up.

I fell asleep. In the morning when Safwan As-Salami passed that way he saw me and recognized me for he had seen me several times before the commandment of veil 'Hijab' (the night Muhammad married Zainab bint Jahsh). He stopped his camel and cried out: "How sad! The wife of the Prophet has been left here!" At this I woke up suddenly and covered my face with my sheet. Without uttering another word he made his camel kneel by me and stood aside while I climbed on to the camel's back. He led the camel by the nose-string and we overtook the caravan at about noon when it had just halted and nobody had yet noticed that I had been left behind.

I learnt afterwards that this incident had been used to slander me. When we reached Medina I fell ill and stayed in bed for more than a month. Though I was quite unaware of it news spread like a scandal in the city and reached the Prophet. I noticed that he did not seem as concerned about my illness as he used to be. He would come, but without addressing me directly, would enquire from others how I was and leave the house.

During my absence the Prophet took counsel with Ali who said, 'O Allah's Messenger, there is no dearth of women; you may, if you like marry another wife. If however you would like to investigate the matter, you may send for her maidservant and enquire into it through her.' The maid servant declared it was all 'rumors and slander'.

One day I felt something decisive was going to happen: the Prophet, my father and mother sat near. The Prophet said: "Aisha, I have heard this and this about you: if you are innocent I expect that Allah will declare your innocence. But if you have committed a sin, you should repent and ask for Allah's forgiveness; when a servant confesses his guilt and repents, Allah forgives him." Hearing these words, the tears dried in my eyes. I looked up to my father expecting that he would reply but he said, "Daughter, I do not know what to say." At last, I said, "You have all heard something about me and believed it. Now if I say I am innocent—and Allah is my witness that I am innocent—you will not believe me; and if I confess something which I never did—and Allah knows that I never did it—you will believe me. I cannot but repeat the words which the father of Joseph (meaning Jacob) has spoken: "I will bear this patiently with good grace." (Koran 12:83). Saying this the state of receiving revelation—convulsion—appeared on the Prophet, when pearl-like drops of perspiration used to gather on his face. We all held our breath and sat silent. When the revelation was over the Prophet seemed overjoyed with happiness, the first words he

175

spoke were: 'congratulations, Aisha, Allah sent down proof of your innocence and then he recited these ten verses."(Saying in short: 'It was all a fib. Those who propagate a baseless fib are doomed to Hell fire.) (Koran 24:11).

It is apparent that Muhammad took the only feasible decision. His love to Aisha, his attachment to Abu Bakr, his tutor, guide and unshakable friend were above all considerations. Once on return from al-Salsal raid, Amr ibn Al-As, the would-be conqueror of Egypt, asked Muhammad: "Who do you love most in this world?" He said, "Aisha." Amr said, "The question is about men." He said, "Aisha's father."

Aisha reported that "in his final illness Muhammad asked his wives: "Where shall I stay tomorrow? Where shall I stay tomorrow?" In fact, he died on the day of my usual turn at my house while his head was between my chest and neck and his saliva was mixed with mine." (Bukhari). It is another addition to the distinction of the 16-year old Aisha that the 62-year old Prophet died on her chest, in her room and was buried in a corner of that room.

Despite all its negative consequences the story of Aisha could be less meaningful to the fate of Muslim women than that of **Zainab bint Jahsh**. This woman was married to Muhammad by a heavenly revelation, with yet another related revelation that brought down women's most hideous plague: the veil or "Hijab."

The story starts with "Zeid bin Haritha, a Christian lad captured by raiders outside his tribe's camp and sold in a Mecca slave market to Khadija. Muhammad asked his wife to grant him "Zaid." He took him to the chiefs of Quraysh and declared him his adopted son and heir and that they were witnesses of that adoption. From that time on Zaid was called "Zaid son of Muhammad." When Zaid's father came to pay a ransom and take him back the boy chose Muhammad over his father and family

Historians never mentioned the purpose of choosing this unfussy and superficial young man to marry a jumpy and sophisticated young women; the story continues:

'When Zaid came of age to be married Muhammad chose for him his cousin Zainab. She was a beautiful Hashemite woman of high rank, edgy temper and aristocratic looks; but Zaid was a slave freed by Muhammad. So Zainab rejected Muhammad's proposal to marry Zaid. In order to serve the purpose and convince her a revelation was in the offing: "It is not fitting for a believer, man or woman, when a matter has been decided by Allah and his Messenger, to have any option about their decision: If anyone disobeys Allah and his Messenger, he is indeed in a clearly wrong path." (Koran 33:36). Facing that divine commandment, Zainab acquiesced and married Zaid and they both moved later to Medina.

It would be redundant to describe the disparity among the newlyweds. Zeid would go to the Prophet complaining in public of Zainab's treatment: "she despises me and talks bad words all the time . . ." Muhammad would, also publicly, warn him: "retain your wife and fear Allah . . ." the complaints were frequent but Zaid would receive the same public warnings.

One day Muhammad went to visit Zaid. Zainab was in the house apparently naked; the wind moved the drape (hijab) hanging at the door. Muhammad saw his daughter-in-law and his heart pounded by her beauty. She asked him to come in. He refused and went talking to himself in a loud voice saying "Praise be to Allah who changes hearts." When Zaid came home Zainab told him about Muhammad's visit and what he said. Zaid went to the Prophet and asked "Shall I divorce Zainab?" "Retain her as your wife and fear Allah," Muhammad answered as always. After that day Zainab treated her husband more callously than ever before until he could take it no more, with the Prophet's permission, he divorced her . . .

Now it was a very difficult situation for Muhammad. He had a burning desire for Zainab for a long time and wanted to marry her but she was his daughter-in-law and there was a clear Koran revelation forbidding believers from marrying in-laws . . . Muhammad needed help that must come from above. At long last, the hard-sell revelation came in the following verses that are recorded in the Koran: "Behold! You did say to one who had received the grace of Allah and *your favor*: "Retain your wife and fear Allah." But you did hide in your heart that which Allah was about to make manifest: you did fear people, but it is more fitting that you should fear Allah. Then when Zaid had dissolved his marriage with her, we joined her in marriage to you in order that (in future) there may be no difficulty to believers in (the matter of) marriage with the wives of their adopted sons, when the latter have dissolved their marriage. (Koran 33:37).

Muhammad made the decision that Zainab should marry Zaid to demonstrate that in Islam there is no difference between classes, but in doing so, either he did not care about Zainab's happiness and satisfaction or, purposefully planned such a temporary and uncertain marriage under the watchful eyes of Khadija. In the process, he committed several errors: 1/ breaking a Koran resolution in not marrying in-laws and amending it, 2/ opening the door for any Muslim to lust after the wife of his kin and marry her after she is divorced, 3/ using Allah's name to satisfy his desire when he claimed that Allah joined him in marriage to Zainab and 4/ using a naïve young man for a specific and premeditated purpose. No wonder that his jealous and voluble wife Aisha repeated to him: "I see your God quickly granting your desires." As to poor Zaid, he migrated in despair to Abyssinia where he regained his Christian faith until he died. Muhammad never asked of him: his name and story were completely ignored by historians.

The wedding party was sumptuous: many guests were invited and lambs stuffed with rice were cooked. The beautiful, *unveiled* bride was sitting in the hall in front of other male guests. When their meal was consummated all well-wishers left except three who came earlier than the others: they sat there looking at pretty Zainab and chatting while Muhammad nervously leaves the hall to Aisha then reenters. He did it three times while the persisting three kept glancing and chatting. Every time, jealous Aisha adds to his torment: "why you are deserting your new folk?" (Women of the Prophet/Dr. Bint el Shati). Before the threesome left a revelation descended: "O you who believe! Enter not the Prophet's houses until leave is given you for a meal, and not so early as to wait for its preparation: but when you are invited, enter; and when you have taken your meal, disperse, without seeking familiar talk. Such annoys the Prophet he is shy to dismiss you, but Allah is not shy to tell the truth. And when you ask ladies for anything you want, *ask them from <u>behind</u> a screen*: that makes for

greater purity for your hearts and for theirs. Nor is it right
for you that you should annoy Allah's Messenger, or that you
should marry his widows after him at any time. Truly such a
thing is in Allah's sight an enormity (Koran 33:53).

Actually the above "Hijab verse" is controversial and
quite misunderstood to the point that Hijab became more an
imposed tradition than a blunt Koran resolution. A tradition to
strengthen that male chauvinism Muslims have inherited across
centuries. The Arabic text says verbatim: "ask them from
<u>behind</u> a screen". The official English Koran translation aptly
says "from <u>before</u> a screen" and for a good reason: should
'screen' mean 'veil'; <u>behind</u> the veil is the woman's face and
not the inquisitor. In addressing a woman, the word 'screen'
means a partition, a divider, a panel or simply a drape if you
use *from behind* as in the Arabic Koranic text and it means
a veil if you use *from before* as in the English translation. So
the most probable meaning of Hijab is screen or panel and not
veil, because in these verses only the Prophet's women in their
homes were meant and not all women out in the open. The
Koran does not specify any veil women should wear outside
their homes. Here comes the <u>wrong interpretation</u> and the
customary generalization all Ulemas have agreed to provide: it
is not the screen, but the veil, anywhere!

To further illustrate that the word "Hijab," according
to the Koranic language as well as the Medina and Mecca
ones meant screen and not veil, we relate the Koran story
of Mary, when: "she withdrew from her family to a place in
the East. She placed a *screen* (hijab in the Arabic text)—*to
screen herself*—from them. Then We sent to her Our angel . . .
(Koran 19:16-17). Mary secluded herself in piety behind a

screen away from the people. It is in the same meaning and for almost a similar purpose that the verse of the hijab was later revealed, dictating that the Prophet's wives should only communicate with strangers from behind a screen, usually a drape or an assembly of canes. The veil known and used today has never been meant or referred to!

On the other hand, to any blunt observer the verse was revealed while the three nosy individuals were enjoying their time chatting and looking at the beautiful bride where the groom was impatiently waiting to enjoy the long-awaited occasion. The verse was, again, highly circumstantial, serving a specific and timely purpose under an extenuating situation. It had served *that* purpose and was fit for *that* situation. Irrespective of its wrong application it should not be taken as a decreed resolution for any woman, anytime.

But the calamity struck and is echoing continuously. From that day on for the first time in the Arabian history, Hijab was imposed on women. Pretty Zainab was partially the culprit: from that day on not only woman's bosoms were covered but her face and legs as well. Islam administered his fatal blow to the Muslim woman, imprisoned her forever behind the veil and pronounced her inexistent in society: wrapped in white or black shrouds from tip to toe, from crib to tomb. Today only those rare, educated and aggressive Muslim women are the exception. They go on swimming against the mainstream threatened with "Kofr"—agnosticism—in life and with hell fire in the hereafter. In 1991 the Prosecutor-General of Iran declared that "anyone who rejects the principle of Hijab is an apostate and the punishment for an apostate under Islamic law is death."

One Saudi princess wrote about her sister when she was ordered by her father to wear the veil: "Sara had been veiling since her menses. The veil stamped her as a *no person* and she soon ceased to speak of her dreams of great accomplishments. She became distant from me and her younger sister who was as yet unconcerned with the institution of veiling. The sharpening of Sara's distance left me longing for the remembered happiness of our shared childhood. It suddenly became apparent to me that happiness is realized only in the face of unhappiness, for I never knew we were so happy until Sara's unhappiness stared me in the face." (Princess, page 27).

When he moved to Medina, Muhammad developed a special addiction to sex in all its aspects: he used to counsel Muslim women on many private sex problems. He preferred natural and unscathed female beauty, including eyebrows' hair that he disallowed removal: "damned are both: who depilates and whose hair is depilated". Passing a woman circumciser he recommended to her: "do not spare but be fair." At one time on return from a raid he asked one of his elderly followers how many women he got. The good man reported he had only one, mother of his children that he loves and cherishes. Muhammad teased him; "how about a young lass you play with as you please?" The good man said: "no thanks, Prophet of Allah, the one I have is enough for me." "He was once sitting among his followers when a pretty maiden passed close by, he got excited and asked leave. When he came back he told the man next to him: one must eliminate evil out, your body has a right on you."(Bedaya & Nehaya). In making love to women he advised Muslims: "Do not approach your women like animals; have between you and them a messenger: the kiss." And, when intercourse is started he recommends "rhythmic and continuous push-ins," (*dahman, dahman*), (Daham or pusher is to this day a favorite man's name in Arabia). With full freedom of selected penetration he advised men: "your women are your tillage; go into your tillage *anyway* you please." Ibn Hisham quoted a Companion saying: "The Prophet would assemble all his wives and make them bend over to the wall and would serve them one after the other" he asked him: "and could he do that?" "Yes, he said, he had the power of thirty men!"

The society Muhammad tried to establish is one that grants men unlimited sexual pleasure using women anyway they please. The most cherished alms Muslim fighters would expect from conquests were white women. When Tareq bin Ziad invaded Spain in 711, he burnt his ships after disembarking and gave his soldiers a historic speech "O people, where to escape? The sea is behind you and the enemy is in front of you . . . You already know what beautiful "houris" this island produces, the daughters of the Greek basking in gems, coral and embroidered silken gowns . . ."

Collecting women though proved disastrous later to the very Muslim future in Iberia and elsewhere. When Muslims crossed the Pyrenees and invaded France the French general Charles Martel asked: "what major war booty Muslims go after" he was told: "women". He withdrew to Poitiers near Paris and ordered as many girls as possible to greet the invaders. Muslims arrived to the war theatre with two armies: the fighting force and the concubines to whom they built a huge camp behind the front line. The morning of the battle shortly before Martel called for the charge, he ordered a special brigade to attack and pilfer the harem camp. News reached the fighters and about half of them rushed back to defend their harem. Chaos ensued; the French showered returning soldiers with arrows, many of them were hit in their backs. When the Muslim general Al-Ghafeqi died by an arrow commotion spread and put the Muslims in disarray. Martel chased the fleeing army through many ambushes back to the Pyrenees, where only a quarter of the invaders gained safety. It is said that the French adage: "cherchez la femme" retorted by Napoleon, was born in Poitiers: a far cry from the Prophet's "women . . . men's mind bogglers". It is also said the Andalusia kingdom was lost to a great extent through women's and concubines' intrigues.

Few years later of daily indulgence with his many women Muhammad started feeling his desert manliness decline. The various and contradicting sexual stories indicate he was suffering a serious sexual disorder: a spermatemphraxis that probably led to priapism: the ability to develop erection without reaching ejaculation. This condition was confirmed by loquacious Aisha supported by Um Sulma: "the Prophet would rise in (the fasting month of) Ramadan after copulation with no seminal fluid (a fasting invalidation) and would kiss some of his wives while fasting without nullifying his fasting because he had the mastery over his penis (literal)."(The Prophet in Ramadan P.12). Poor Aisha and Um Sulma, they ill-diagnosed their husband: what they considered miraculous was in fact disastrous.

As soon as he felt his deficiency he started worrying about his young and beautiful wives from the many intruders and trespassers. As any political leader's house, his was wide open to people of all ranks and colors. After Aisha's "Ifk" and Zainab's wedding night incidents, he started showering his—and other women—with hot and uncompromising verses: "O you, who believe, do not enter houses other than yours until you have asked permission and saluted those in them; that is best for you in order that you may heed. If you find nobody in the house, do not enter until permission is given to you, if you are asked to go back, go back. That makes for greater purity for yourselves; and Allah knows well whatever you do. Say to the believing men that they should lower their gazes and guard their organs (literal); that will make for greater purity for them. And Allah is well acquainted with all that they do. And say to the believing women that they should lower their gazes and guard their organs (literal); that they should not display their beauty and ornaments except what appears thereof; and they should draw their lapels over their bosoms and not display their beauty except to their husbands, their fathers, their husbands' fathers, their sons, their husbands' sons or their women or the slaves whom their right hands possess or emasculated male servants or small children unexposed yet to women's organs. And they should not strike their feet (Domloj) to draw attention to their hidden ornaments. O you believers repent to Allah so you may succeed." (Koran 24: 27).

What tormenting anxiety reverberates in these verses? The ailing Prophet was so jealous and concerned about his women he even choked them with more ruthless verses: "O consorts of the Prophet, if any of you were guilty of evident misconduct, the punishment would be doubled on her, and that is easy for Allah." (Koran 33:30). He also authorized his followers: "As to those women on whose part you fear disloyalty and ill-conduct, admonish them, refuse to share their beds, and *beat* them (Koran 4:34). Just a *suspicion* of disloyalty in a wife is justification for the husband to *beat her!*

Such was the downgrading path Muslim women were subjected to since Jahilyia. It is a wrong and baseless testimonial to keep repeating that Islam elevated them to higher ranks. Dr. Souad Al-Sabah the leading intellectual lady in modern Kuwait says: "Democracy is when a woman can talk of her lover without anybody killing her". A Muslim woman today has no face or identity. At age 9 she is considered an adult eligible to marriage and for any wrong doing she can be incarcerated. She is not equal to men: "Men are the managers of the affairs of women because Allah has preferred men over women and women were expended of their rights". (Koran 4:34) Islam believes and promotes only one relationship between male and female and that is the relation of sex and lust. Muhammad said: "If a man and a woman are alone in one place, the third person present is the devil." A woman is not allowed to swim, ski, ride a bike, dance, practice gymnastics, or any other sport.

She is to be treated by female doctors and dentists. Not allowed to practice birth control or have abortions; carrying an illegitimate child means she has to die. She is worth half of a man. It doesn't matter who she is, how educated and what is her earning potential. The cash fine for murdering a woman intentionally or unintentionally is half as much as for a man. Blood money or "dieh", a sum paid to the next of kin as compensation for the murder of a relative, is twice as much in the case of a murdered man as in the case of a woman. Her testimony in a court of law is equal to half of that of a man.

In most countries she doesn't vote and may not be elected to office. She inherits only half as much as her male siblings.

She cannot get custody of her children; even if their father dies. In the case of divorce or death she surrenders her children to their father and/or his family. She cannot travel or work without her father or husband's permission. A sad paradox in Saudi Arabia lately is one lady pilot who earned her jet flying license but may still not drive her car from the airport!

A woman cannot choose her mate and is not permitted to divorce him if things did not work out. She has to meet all her husband's desires especially the sexual ones. If she refuses he has the right to deny her food, shelter and livelihood.

A Muslim woman should endure any violence or torture imposed on her by her husband for she is fully at his disposal. Ex-wife of Omar Sharif and famous movie star of Egypt Faten Hamama, tackled this sinister problem in her film "I Seek a Solution". Without man's permission a woman may not leave her house even to visit her parents. Otherwise her prayers and devotions will not be accepted by Allah and curses of heaven and earth will fall upon her. Her husband can divorce her without her knowledge for any reason of his and is required to support her for only 100 days thereafter. If he dies she is entitled to a meager eighth of his fortune. She can only ask for divorce if her husband is impotent (usually difficult to prove) or if he does not have sex with her at least one night in every forty nights. A Sunna husband can have four permanent wives and a Shia as many temporary wives as he wants. In many countries they perform "Khitan" circumcision to subdue her desire and climax: a fatal blow in fact to the majority of men unable to bring their debilitated wives to orgasm!

Is this the right reward a Muslim woman should get in her life? This question—and appeal is addressed to all Ulemas and clerics who have read these lines so far and focused their moral integrity not incensed spirit: is this how you conscientiously want your sisters, wives and mothers to be treated? Isn't this female your other half in society? And haven't your society been flying so far—among other world communities—with one wing only? How do you lament every day your lack of progress and pass the buck on oppressing Western nations when you cripple this very half by your own hands? It is the Holy Scripture you would say, you cannot trespass its prescribed parameters, it has been written and no deviation is allowed. Are you satisfied with your prescribed fate: what is written is written and your nation is bound to continue living its third Jahilyia?

This woman is not only your pleasure object or reproducing machine but your life companion, the mother of your children and the goddess of your house. She is not that stupid female "devoid of brain and creed" the Prophet described in an elusive moment under Jahilyia-like circumstances. She is rather what the most quoted Arab poet Ahmad Shawqi said:

> **"A mother is a school; when you well prepare . . .**
> **You would build a nation whose likes are rare!"**

This and similar women supporting voices, to the satisfaction of many observers, are now resounding across the Muslim world. Young girls are acquiring modern education that is proving detrimental to traditional tyrannies although cultural and tribal customs still seclude many Arab women in the name of Islam, while other traditions do not. In Indonesia, which is more than 90 percent Muslim, women are unveiled. One area of West Sumatra is matriarchal. The Islam that has emerged in Indonesia of the moderate Shafi School is very different from the more stringent Wahhabi Islam in Saudi Arabia.

Western-educated women of the Islamic world are not usually happy to be back in their Islamic societies. They pay the price for leaving behind the emphasis on feminine allure in much of the western lifestyle, dress, entertainment and behavior. Many maintain the freedoms of the West. In an elegant pink Pakistani outfit in Islamabad, Oxford-educated Rehana Hyder said: "Things are changing in Pakistan. Women are certainly freer."

Devout Muslims know that Prophet Muhammad is reported to have said, "Of all actions permitted by Allah, divorce is the least tolerable." Those devout however still reject "women's lib" and "equality" as per Western concepts. They agree however to bestow Islamic guarantees of women's status based on equality, inheritance, laws and other legal rights. While most Muslim countries take a conservative view of women, those educated females are marking their points day after day even in the shadow of the Islamist movements. Slowly but surely, the humiliating verses and sayings of the Prophet against women are being transgressed. The Islamic revival "Sahwa" is well and alive though scattered and too damn slow!

SEVENTEEN

Terrorism in Islam

"I was sent by the sword. The good is with the sword, the good is in the sword, the good is by the sword. My followers will be always good as long as they carry the sword."

Muhammad

Many scholars insist that Islam relied on peaceful expansion and that armed jihad was only authorized in cases of self-defense. This theory ignores entirely the doctrines developed by all texts of the

Koran and Sinna. Here are some hadith from Bukhari, Muslim and other trusted traditionalists:

"Verily Allah has purchased of the believers their lives and their properties; for theirs (in return) is Paradise. They fight in His cause, so they kill and get killed . . ." (Bukhari), and:

"Allah's Messenger said, "Know that Paradise is under the shades of swords." (Abdullah bin Abi Auf), and:

"Narrated Abu Huraira (a Prophet Companion): I heard Allah's Messenger saying, "The example of a Mujahid in Allah's cause—and Allah knows better who really strives in His cause—is like a person who fasts and prays continuously. Allah guarantees that He will admit the Mujahid in His Cause into Paradise if he is killed, otherwise He will return him to his home safely with rewards and war booty." (Bukhari).

When Muhammad found later in the Aws and Khazraj of Medina natural foes to Quraysh and them in him a readily acceptable Prophet he employed the new situation to his best advantage. His returning followers joined some members of the two tribes in arms. His newfound forces gathered momentum and surrounded him as impenetrable ramparts. They emboldened him to recap the ancient list of all those who mocked, harassed and hurt him in Mecca with a new list of those in Medina and decided to eliminate them one after the other.

To achieve this purpose along with other regular army raids, he established his "Saraya", a plural for "Sariya" from "Sara" or night travel. Saraya were detachments of one or more trained killers to assume covert assassination missions under night darkness. This terror tactic achieved a double purpose: eliminating for good old and persistent enemies and sowing terror to arraign people to the safe haven of Islam.

To the western reader this is a gross and disgusting dealing unbefitting a Prophet holding a Godly message in his other hand. But one should remember that Islam did not deviate much from the Jahilyia era and all survival means inherent to its hungry desert wolves. Westerners consistently misunderstood the rhetoric and actions emanating from that part of the world. In their misguided efforts to be inclusive and tolerant they have glossed over the basics of Islam, attempting (unwittingly) to see this religion through the glasses of a culture still steeped in Judeo-Christian assumptions. Muhammad acted in pure Jahilyia philosophy to impose his message, a behavior that no matter how strange it appears today was quite acceptable in those days and still adaptable now: "support your brother Muslim whether oppressor or oppressed."

There is no question that many Arabs and Muslims vocally decry terrorism; but the majority rejoices in the success of any terrorist attack and thanks Allah for it. The Islamic community does not confront the terrorists nor oppose their interpretation of Islam; simply because they know it is *the true interpretation*. They distance themselves from terrorist acts but do not excommunicate the perpetrators. As long as they do not confront them they should not blame others for their reactions nor should they complain that "the non-Muslims are misinterpreting Islam" and are biased and islamophobic.

Hereunder are some narrated samples of disparate Saraya acts:

From his moderate and reconciliatory Mecca stance where Muhammad said: "Whoever hurts a Zimee (a Jew or a Christian protected by the Islamic state) he would be like hurting me and who hurts me, he hurts God," in Medina he unleashed his 'firsts' on the Jews: "kill any Jew you can lay your hands on." (Ibn Ishaq and al-Waqidi). Thereupon Muhaysa bin Masud leapt upon Ibn Sunayna, a Jewish merchant with whom they had social and business relations, and killed him. His elder brother who was not a Muslim at the time began to beat him, saying, 'you enemy of God, did you kill him when much of the fat on your belly comes from his wealth?' Muhaysa answered, 'had the one who ordered me to kill him ordered me to kill you I would have cut your head off."

The second terrorist incident involves another on Muhammad's request: to murder an old Jewish man named Abu Afak who put out a poem criticizing Muhammad and urging his fellow Medinans to probe him. Muhammad said, "Who will deal with this rascal for me?" A Sariya by Salim Ibn Umayr who had participated in the battle of Badr was organized, he said, 'I take a vow that I shall either kill Abu Afak or die before him.' He waited for an opportunity until a hot night came and Abu Afak slept in an open place. Salim knew it, he tiptoed himself in and placed his sword on his liver and pressed it till it reached his bed. The enemy of Allah screamed and his followers rushed to him, took him to his house and interred him." (Tabacat Al-Ayian).

The third incident involves Muhammad's demand to murder a woman named Asma bint Marwan who was a poetess. When Abu Afak had been killed she displayed disaffection. Blaming Islam and its followers; her poem said:

194

"I despise Malik, al-Nabit, Aus and Khazraj (*)
You obey a stranger to you, not of Murad or Muzhaj. (**)
Do you expect good from him after killing your leaders?
Like a hungry man waiting for food and feeders?
Is there no man of pride who would surprise and attack him?
And cut off hopes of those who expect nil from him?"

* Major Medina Arab tribes ** Jewish tribes

Hassan bin Thabit, The Prophet's poet/defender answered her:

"Banu Wa'il, Waqif and Khatma (*) are inferior to Khazraj.
When she called for folly woe to her in her weeping,
Death was shortly coming and is slowly creeping.
She stirred up a mighty man (**) of glorious origin,
Noble in his going out and in his coming in . . .
He dyed her in her blood just before midnight
Incurring no guilt whatsoever in this plight"

(*) Medina Jewish tribes. (**) Muhammad.

Hassan's response wasn't enough. The Prophet said to his retine, "Who will rid me of Marwan's daughter?" Umayr al-Khatmi who was with him volunteered and that very night he sneaked to her house. Her children were sleeping around her with one whom she was suckling. He thrust his sword in her chest till it pierced down to her back. Then fled and offered the dawn prayers in the mosque with the Prophet. In the morning he came and told Muhammad what he had done, who said, "O Umayr, you have helped Allah and His Messenger." When he asked if he would have to bear any evil

195

consequences the Prophet said, "Two goats won't butt their heads for her", so Umayr went back to his people satisfied." (Al-Waqidi)

"Now there was a great commotion among Khatma that day about the affair of bint Marwan. She had five sons and when Umayr went to them from the Prophet he said, "I have killed bint Marwan, O sons of Khatma, withstand me if you can; don't keep me waiting." That was the first day Islam became powerful among Khatma; who became Muslims because they saw the power of Islam." (Al-Waqidi).

Other similar acts were performed and executed. Any reader, Muslim or otherwise who sees extreme oddities in those acts, should realize that Muslims are not directed to compromise when it comes to fight for or defend Islam. A son of Abu Bakr, the Caliph who had learned lots of tolerance from Waraka, was fighting on the side of the Meccans before embracing Islam. He one day said to his father: "You know, at Badr you were twice under my sword. But my love for you held back my hand." "Son," remarked Abu Bakr, "if I had that chance only once you must have been no more." (Al-Waqidi).

All Saraya campaigns today like in the past, carry such religious vehemence. This of course includes the various raids of al-Qaeda. Modern examples abound like the story of David Belfield a Baptist young man from Long Island who came to Washington to study at Howard University. Under the influence of an Iranian Muslim David embraced Islam, changed his name to Daoud Salahuddin and became increasingly devout. His Iranian handler had little trouble persuading him to kill a man he had never met: Ali Akbar Tabatabai who lived in Bethesda, Maryland and who was the chief spokesman in the United States for the counter-revolutionary forces against the Khomeini government. Daoud saw the act as an Islamic duty and assassinated Tabatabai. He fled to Canada and then to Tehran. The Iranian government had agreed to send him to China to study medicine. The rest of his story was never known.

A Western military campaign is welcome if it serves the Muslim cause like in Kosovo or Iraq. Islam considers this a God's gift: "Blessed He who subjugated this to us that we were not anticipating". For years Muslims were ever thankful to America for eliminating Saddam and ever resentful and confrontational for occupying this Muslim country; they would see this as an assault on Islam. Likewise the U.S. may receive verbal assurances from Muslim governments supporting the fight against Islamic terrorists but the public support will not be there especially over an extended period of time.

To further understand this controversy one should note that all social, political, economic, and religious systems are subsumed under Islam. Not one Muslim today dare contradict any aspect of life depicted in the Koran, the Hadith and the Sharia. These are the faith parameters; although most of them were incidentals in a bygone era they still remain sacred assumptions. Muslims believe Islam is true and Christianity is false. They believe in Christ and glorify Him in as much as they despise his followers. Muhammad threw a fleeting principle for all Muslims to follow that turned out to their disadvantage: "contradict (in ways, means and lifestyle) the Jews and the Christians". A tremendous dilemma to any

Muslim immersed up to his neck in western daily life and a valid reason why Muslim nations are relatively unsuccessful in comparison to the 'infidel nations of the West'. Many see this disparity as an attack on the veracity of their faith and a continual source of frustration. Ayatollah Khomeini decrying the impact of foreign medicines in Iran declared, ". . . Our leaders have forgotten our traditional medicine and encouraged a handful of inexperienced young men to study this cursed European medicine. Today we realize that illnesses such as typhus, typhoid fever and the like are curable only by traditional remedies."

Muslims will all unite in their joint detestation to the Christians and Jews. The amazing thing is that they don't bear any of this against the Buddhists for example simply because the Koran does not mention them. Muslims are raised from early childhood to revere the Prophet Muhammad and honor him highly. They are commanded to hold his honor dearer than their own lives or those of their family members. Even "secular" Muslims who do not practice Islam hardly ever perform the daily prayers and live a thoroughly non-religious life will jolt immediately—of course only in public—when confronted with any critique of the person of Muhammad. It would be worse than an insult to their persons. The latest "cartoon uprising" against the west is a palpable example.

Muslims may harbor animosity towards one another in more sordid ways than with the infidels. Again, this is engendered by a fleeting ruling by Muhammad: "he, who identifies flagrancy (among Muslims) should rectify it by his hand, if unable, by his word, if unable, by his heart and this is the least of faith." This is an open invitation to the interference of any Muslim into any other Muslim's life and affairs whenever he deems it 'flagrancy' according to his own level of understanding and rectify it by whatever means he sees fit. Hence we see today many self-appointed groups of "Takfir"—apostatizers—who may pronounce any open minded Muslim an apostate and condemn him to death. The religious police "Motawa" of Saudi Arabia are an official application of that resolution.

Muslims were armed in the past with swords and Koran verses to fight each other and achieve political objectives. Similar scenarios took place recently in Algeria and still ongoing in various other countries. The "Apostatizers" form a relentless movement in every Muslim country to control Muslims' behavior and constantly commands them to follow the Prophet's "way of life" and basic Islamic laws. Murdering others in Islam's name is part of that style and system. Muslims loosen much of their desire for blood upon their Muslim brethren . . . it's the spirit of Islam. Those who are not Muslim enough are the first to feel its blades. In this respect the French philosopher Renan observed: "Muslims are the first victims of Islam." Many non-Muslims are also victims in the process. Innocents are murdered by radicals who are developing more sophisticated terror methods against those who are not of their ilk.

Many Muslims around the world are peace-loving and thoroughly disgusted about the acts of Islamic terrorism. Those however do not know the basic facts about their own religion. These lines have been written to expose them to the facts and incite them to denounce terrorism knowingly. Muslim terrorists are usually well-educated in Islam, profoundly pious and generally spiritual leaders. They do what they do and how they do it with strong conviction of following the example of their Prophet. It is instructive to note that Muhammad's first military victory was accomplished during a month of truce which he broke by raiding a caravan. From then on the same example was followed when the three "Khawarej" murderers went out seeking the lives of Moawia, Ali and Amr inside their mosques in the most sacred month of Ramadan. Today the same sacred month is the preferred time for any such prowess.

The good Muslims who revoke terrorism without expressing it are always in deep dilemma. They cannot protest, revolt or even criticize for a valid reason: Muhammad was not only content to conquer by force or kill those that merely opposed him verbally, he also taught that Muslims who leave the Islamic faith are to be murdered as well. Here are again some quotes from Bukhari's collection of Hadith: "Allah's Messenger said, "The blood of a Muslim who confesses that none has the right to be worshipped but Allah and that I am His Messenger cannot be shed except in three cases: in Qasas (punishment) for murder, a married person who commits illegal sexual intercourse and the one who reverts (Apostates) from Islam and leaves the Muslims."

In this context even when fearless Caliph Omar himself was called by his friend Abu Bakr into Islam he was extremely cautious. He knew Islam was a one-way street with no exit. The big man wanted time to consider all the underlying hazards and opportunities. He only took decision when he was certain his big future lied there and in the offing. Later Omar was the hawk who emboldened Muhammad to go the merciless road. He once narrated: "the day of the battle of Badr, Allah defeated the invaders; seventy of them were killed and seventy captive. The Prophet counseled Abu Bakr, Ali and I about the captives. Abu Bakr said: 'Prophet of God these are our cousins and kin; I see that we collect ransoms from them; this way we strengthen our finances and probably win them as future supporters'. The Prophet said: 'what do you say, Omar?' I said: 'By Allah I don't see what Abu Bakr saw. I rather request you to give me Abu Safian to cut his head and Give Hamza his brother Al-Abbas to cut his head and give Ali his brother Akeel to cut his head, so it shall be known to all that we have no mercy on these pagans and these are their leaders!" Muhammad agreed later with Abu Bakr but such was the approach of Omar and his terror tradition throughout his Caliphate.

Ikrima (historian) narrated: "Some atheists (apostates) were brought to Ali and he burnt them. The news of this event reached Ibn Abbas (a Companion) who said, "If I had been in his place I would not have burnt them as Allah's messenger forbade it, saying, "Do not punish anybody with Allah's punishment (fire)." I would have killed them according to the statement of Allah's messenger, "Whoever changed his Islamic religion, then kill him.""

Ali did not comment on the critique to his sentence but supported the capital punishment on all renegades: "Whenever I tell you a Hadith from Allah's messenger, by Allah, I would rather fall down from the sky than ascribe a false statement to him; but if I tell you something between me and you, (not a Hadith) then it was indeed a trick (i.e., I may say things just to cheat my enemy). No doubt I heard Allah's messenger saying, "during the last days there will appear some young foolish people who will say the best words but their faith will not go beyond their throats (pretend their faith) and will go out from their religion as an arrow goes out of the game. So wherever you find them kill them, for whoever kills them shall have reward on the Day of Resurrection." Not only did Muhammad teach that Muslims are to murder those that have left Islam, "wherever you find them", he further taught that a Muslim who commits this type of murder will be doing God's service and be rewarded!

Hence the waged 'War on Apostates' after the death of the Prophet by Caliph Abu Bakr was unforgiving. The first to re-conquer was Taghleb. Only this time the options were Islam or the sword; their plea to pay taxes and keep their religion was not accepted in line with the Prophet's deathbed will; their Christian shrines and heritage were demolished and Abu Bakr ordered their conqueror to 'stay with them six months and make sure their Islamization was complete.' Many extremists today would love to perform this duty hoping that Paradise would be the reward. Any renegade apostate must be eliminated, a recent example is writer Selman Rushdie whose blood was legitimized by a Fatwa from Khomeini; he was kept alive by a special British security force until Khomeini's death whereby a reversal to the Fatwa was given.

What Muslims should accept today is that many of the Jahilyia ways and means committed by the Prophet and his followers quite acceptable to the old existing norms, do not fit the 21st Century's civilizations where man's rights are sacred. Old Sarayas sent under dark to liquidate people in their sleep because of satire and contradicting views are very much similar to many terror actions today. They operate secretly and murder without law or justice those who merely disagree or even verbally oppose them. Such Islamic "traditions" are not compatible with those of the world community in the age of globalization but a practice that negatively affects Islamic societies first and foremost. It relates to what we have seen done in countries such as Algeria, Iran, Iraq, Tunisia, Lybia and Egypt. The end result has been brutal massacres, murders and tortures.

The West does not know what every Muslim scholar knows; that the worst enemies of Islam are from within. Today's fundamentalists are the still-existing yesteryears' fanatics who delude others by the deeply dyed religious exterior they display. The Prophet, along with Ali, had his share with them, "When you see them pray, you will consider your own prayers insignificant. They recite the Koran but it does not exceed the limits of their throat." (Hadith.) The outward religious appearance and character of the fanatics deluded thousands in the past and continue to delude people today. Muslims should be aware that their mere fanatic adherence to the fundamental aspects of Islam is enough to turn them to extremists of the worst type.

Today's fundamentalist groups are platforms of the restless and orthodox Islamic thinking around the world. They and other Muslims believe themselves to be on the leading edge of a general revival of interest in Islam—a widespread determination to turn away from Western atheism and materialism to purer Islamic governance. Iran was the first country where fundamentalist thinkers have succeeded in overthrowing a secular, westernized leader. Lybia, Tunisia and Egypt launched the "Arab Spring" instigated by the USA. Success or failures of such regimes remains anybody's guess.

Where are the "human rights" if Islam denies freedom of speech to others, how does that reflect upon Islam and what we see occurring in the Islamic world today? And why the more religious Muslim nations become, the more oppressive they are toward all basic human rights? Simple: because they dwell deeper into the circumstantial axioms of the faith and apply them verbatim today! Take the Taliban for instance. They had been accomplished Muslim idealists and great fighters. But once in power, ideals gave way to fundamentalism: they began to oppress the populace specifically women. Initially they said it was only temporary but it has continued to get worse for Afghani women as time passed. Taliban's was an updated copy of the true and veritable Medina Islam.

Many Muslims believe they have lost track of their theological teaching. Islam has been hijacked by the discourse of anger and the rhetoric of rage. Clerics have allowed for too long their pulpits to become bully pulpits in which people with often recognizable psychopathology use anger. This is a very powerful emotion that irks Muslims up with a bitter and spiteful feeling towards other people who are completely unaware of the conditions in the Muslim world or the oppressive assaults of some Western countries on Muslims. Those clerics have lost their bearings because they only single out the radical, outlandish approach of their faith. All theologians in the entire Muslim world are free lancers accountable only to themselves.

Very few, perilously liberated voices emanate using reason and speaking freely. Abdul Rahman Alrashed, Al-Arabyia T.V. chief declared in London after the Beslan massacre in Russia: "Our terrorist sons are an end-product of our corrupted *culture*. The painful truth is that most perpetrators of suicide operations in buses, schools and residential buildings around the world for the past 10 years have been Muslims." He said: "if Muslims want to change their image they must admit the scandalous facts rather than disparage critics or justify terrorists' behavior." Moderate Islamic clerics and thinkers in an effort to dispel what made violence integral to Islam should follow this example and denounce other clerics who preach hate and call for the destruction of the Christians and Jews. In a continuous reconciliatory move the western media go out of their way to cover up the obvious; preferring words such as "militants" and "extremists" and often refusing to identify the religious motivations.

In an effort to shine their pictures among themselves and world communities Muslim states today resort to a culture of double-faced rhetoric. The important thing is to say what your listeners want to hear more than telling the truth in line with Muhammad's words. "If you are plagued by wrongdoings, cover up". Words are more important than ideas and ideas more important than facts. It is this trait that caused many westerners to wonder how such eccentric statements can be made that are patently false. In fights, people claim victory before anything started; the words and ideas are embraced while the facts are not important. This mentality is exhibited most powerfully all the time. Muslims are traditional enemies to both logic and truth. The veiled truth—like the veiled woman—is what they grew accustomed with.

It is naïve to believe that terrorism can be eliminated and optimistic to think that the West can contain it. When fanaticism is fueled by religious fervor it breeds a disease with no military or political cure. At the same old steps of Muhammad Islam's war is waged to establish its supremacy when every other argument to convince those who reject it fails. Jihad in every aspect including terrorism is then dutiful and justifiable. Hence, the world of Islam is in a state of perpetual struggle against Muslims and non-Muslims. Fundamentalists believe and preach that defying their teaching is defiance to Allah's authority. In their perspective of Islamic law "non-believers in Islam should be treated as a sort of cancerous growth on the organism of humanity . . . that is necessary to remove by any surgical means in order to save the rest of humanity." On the other hand considering what has happened in many Muslim countries, it appears that cancerous growths within Islam also abound and are causing much more deaths than outside it.

For reasons beyond the desire to curb terrorism, Christians should renew their efforts to introduce Muslims to the Spirit of Peace. This may not stop future waves of terror but may close one major accessible avenue. The Clash of Civilizations will intensify and violence will escalate between Muslims and Jews in Israel, Hindus in India, Buddhists in Burma and Catholics in the Philippines. Islam lives in bloody confrontations within and without its borders. At the time of writing these lines Muslims see their most sacred land in Arabia, the second most sacred shrines in Iraq and the third most sacred shrine in Palestine occupied by infidels or infidel-aided infidels. Muslims who do not possess sophisticated weapons to brazen out the West resort to the only two available weapons: their bodies and their explosives.

The totalitarian nature of Islam is nowhere more apparent than in the concept of jihad whose ultimate aim is to conquer the entire world and submit it to the one true faith: the law of Allah. Islam alone has been granted the truth: there is no possibility of salvation outside it. It is the sacred, incumbent religious duty established in the Koran and the Traditions of all Muslims to bring it to all humanity. Such is the initial planning of the Founding Fathers to proclaim Jihad as a divine institution enjoined for the sacred purpose of advancing Islam. Therefore Muslims must strive, fight and kill in the name of God. Ibn Khaldun, the foremost Arab historian/philosopher said: "In the Muslim community the holy war is a *religious duty* because of the universalism of the Muslim mission and the *obligation* to convert everybody either by persuasion or by force." (Preface 13). This totalitarian nature is nowadays costing adherents lots of damage and suffering. The present Islamic awakening "Sahwa" is unfortunately fuelled by verses of the Medina and Othman Koran. A corrective spiritual revolution is due to redirect Muslims to the early Mecca haven of tolerance and accommodation. There lies the salute of Islam and its followers.

Many Muslims and Christians have left or fled their homes in the Middle East and North Africa because in Islamic societies they were either directly persecuted or at best second class citizens. They have come to the West because they were longing for freedom and the desire to be absolutely loyal citizens. More Muslims have left their oppressed countries to live in societies built on Christian values that do not discriminate on race, culture or religion even when attacked by *some* people from one specific group. Yet while championing human rights around the world caution should be taken to monitor Muslim communities as Muhammad's commendation would always ring in their brains: "play the meek until you have the upper hand . . ." and to keep in mind that the more religious a Muslim becomes the more he espouses hatred and fanaticism. All Muslims eventually need to deal with the history and sources of their religion. It is only fair to calmly ask them to give a second look on the teachings of the Koran regarding war against unbelievers that belong to yesteryears including the examples Muhammad had set in dealing with his critics and dissenters. Here lies the narrow door to a large and successful avenue of Christian/Islamic dialogues.

The Western media while producing many vile programs on Islam has also produced and aired material of the highest quality with a high level of accuracy only to be sneered at by Muslims as not good enough. Where is the counteracting Muslim media? Where are its spokespeople, scholars and literary figures? The truth is they don't show up because those individuals are torn between a fundamental dogma they cannot deviate from and a liberal belief they cannot express. Instead of looking inward and asking painful questions they take the simple way out by attacking people whom Allah tells them will do mean things, say bad things and plot against them.

A word that recurs in radical Muslim proclamations is "dignity." That is not a political demand, nor one that can be achieved through negotiation. Indeed they see a conspiracy by the West to steal this dignity. For groups that feel victimized negotiation with a powerful adversary can itself be demeaning. The Muslim demand for respect isn't something that can be negotiated; but that doesn't mean the West shouldn't take it seriously. For as the Muslim world gains a greater sense of dignity in its Western interfacing, the destructive weapons of Iran, Al-Qaeda and Hamas will lose much of its potency.

Conspiracy or not, Ulemas are to blame for the terrible backlash against Muslims. The simple reason is that when a crazy Christian does something terrible everyone in the West knows it is the actions of a mad man because they have some knowledge of the core beliefs and ethics of Christianity. When a mad Muslim does something evil or foolish the West assumes it is from the religion of Islam because they don't see a Muslim stand to voice a constructive opinion condemning wrongdoers; they simply take it for granted that Islam's teachings and Asabyia prevent him to do so.

The common problem that runs through the West's battles with militant Islam is how to resolve a confrontation with an adversary that appears unable or unwilling to negotiate. implacability may have been the most important lesson so far. Great issues of war and peace will be resolved by God's will, not by human negotiators. With God secured on their side Islamists don't often compromise. Better to lose than to bargain with the devil. Better to suffer physical hardship than humiliation. This blockage is always evident in any conflict with Muslim groups. Al-Qaeda doesn't seek negotiations or a political settlement nor should the West imagine it could reach one with a group that insists America and its allies should withdraw altogether from the Muslim world.

EIGHTEEN

Antagonism
with the Christians

*"And remember, Jesus, the son of Mary, said:
"O children of Israel: I am the messenger of
Allah to you confirming the Torah before me,
and giving glad tidings of a messenger to come
after me, whose name shall be Ahmed . . ."*

Koran 61:6.

Many Muslims and a sizeable amount of Christians fail to track down the foundation of the intense yet mostly undisclosed antagonism by the followers of Islam towards Christians. While Jesus is the most glorified prophet in the Koran his followers are infidels, subject to Jihad in the world and hellfire in the hereafter.

The downcast reason for this enmity is the Koran Medina verse above quoting Jesus as saying that Muhammad (Ahmad) is the next—and final—messenger after him. Christians are convinced beyond any shadow of doubt that there is no mention of Ahmad and no prophecy concerning him in the Gospels. Consequently they believe the Koran is definitely feigning that.

This is perhaps the direst negative feeling afflicting Muslims. While they exalt Christ in their daily prayers, they feel betrayed and let down by the Christians who denied them simple acceptance of Muhammad's prophesy: the backbone and most fundamental pillar of their belief. Hence the Koran reasserts on its own that "Muhammad is . . . the Messenger of Allah and the Seal of the Prophets." (Koran 3:85). And in a further bombarding assault on the non-Muslims it states: "If anyone desires a religion other than Islam, never will it be accepted from him; and in the hereafter he will be in the ranks of the losers." (Koran 33:40).

In recent years this trend gained momentum when an alleged "Barnabas Gospel" was "discovered" and released in Pakistan confirming Ahmad's advent after Jesus to be the 'seal of the prophets'. Soon enough the manuscript has been pronounced false as written in Spain the 16th century by a monk from Muslim Arab origin whose elders converted to

Christianity to save their skins. The Christian refutation to its authenticity further inflamed this issue.

The final blow in this respect is "Alfatiha" or opener, the Koran's prologue that is essential to Muslims as "Our Father . . ." to the Christian; it is repeated about 30 times a day during prayers and in solemn occasions like weddings or mourning: "In the name of Allah, most gracious, most merciful. Praise be to Allah, cherisher and sustainer of the worlds; most gracious, most merciful; master of the Day of Judgment. You do we worship, and Your aid we seek. Show us the straight way; *the way of those on whom you bestowed your grace, those whose (portion) is not wrath, and who go not astray.*" (Koran, English version 1.1-6). The Arabic text of the last verse does not replicate this mild and reconciliatory translation. It rather says: "The way of those on whom you bestowed your grace, <u>not</u> *those disgraced or those who went astray*". The latter two categories are the Jews and the Christians. They are inserted by name in the official interpretation and taught in schools or preached across pulpits. Here we stop to ask the question: what negative feelings of antagonism can a Muslim carry towards Christians while repeating this prayer knowing what it means and to whom it is addressed!

To add fuel to fire all four Gospels agree that Jesus invariably said: "False Christs and false prophets shall rise (after me) and shall show signs and wonders . . ." (Mark 13.22). A detrimental and pestering situation when Islam and the Koran even confirm Jesus' second coming to proclaim the hour of judgment: "and Jesus shall be a sign for the hour of judgment; therefore have no doubt about the hour . . ."

(Koran 43.61.) This dilemma arouses Muslim clerics to declare in revenge that: 1/ the Gospels were not originally compiled by men but words of God revealed to Jesus, thus asserting the likewise Koranic texts and: 2/ the originally revealed Gospels vanished and were replaced by existing man-made tempered documents to offset the authenticity of that particular Koran verse and the prophesy of Muhammad.

In a further assault on the Christians and in order to confirm them as infidels the Koran attacks their belief in a Triune God, accusing them of 'Shirk' or polytheism for considering Jesus 'the Son of God equal to him in essence.' A particular short Sura was especially devoted to contradict such Christian belief: "Say He is Allah the one and only, Allah the absolute, He begot not nor is He begotten and there is none like unto Him" (Koran 112.1-4) The Original Mecca Koran and the 'Gospel according to Hebrews' both supports this assertion. It creates a debatable issue worth addressing for the sake of an Islamic/Christian rapprochement.

Muslim clerics with a measure of a non-judgmental attitude should agree it is unthinkable that the Gospels were purposely falsified to offset a Jesus prophesy regarding Ahmad simply because similar manuscripts of the same Gospels dating back to pre-Islamic eras are still in existence in many languages and hold the same contemporary texts. As to the Triune God or the various aspects of the one Deity a special examination is due to similarities in the Torah, the Gospels and even the Koran.

The Old Testament uses the plural name of Deity: "And God said, let us make man in our image, after our likeness . . . so God created man in His own image (Genesis 1:26, 27).

And: "Also I heard the voice of the Lord, saying, whom I shall send, and who will go for us? (Isaiah 6:8). Here we have to notice the two words, "I" and "us." For the One who says "I" says also "us." That indicates—if you add the ever existing Holy Spirit, the oneness of God under three various aspects.

When the Torah was revealed it was not customary for kings of great empires to use the word "we" in magnifying themselves. King Nebuchadnezzar the Emperor of Babylonia issued a decree saying, "Therefore I make a decree . . ." (Daniel 3:29). King Darius issued a decree saying, "I make a decree . . ." (Daniel 6:26). So when God uses the words "we" or "us," it is not to magnify Himself but to indicate that He is a Triune God. The book of Psalms offers a clear demonstration: "The LORD said *unto my Lord*, sit you at my right hand, until I make your enemies your footstool." Jesus argued this passage with the Pharisees saying: "What think you of Christ? Whose son is He? They say unto him, the son of David. He said unto them, how then does David in spirit call him Lord, saying, "the LORD said unto my Lord, sit you on my right hand, till I make your enemies thy footstool" (Mat.22:42). The only right interpretation for this passage is the belief in the triune God. For in this passage we see "The LORD" is God the Father and "my Lord" is God the Son. David, by the Spirit, called Him Lord and that Spirit is the "Holy Spirit."

On the occasion of the baptism of Jesus by John the Baptist we see clearly the Triune God. "When He had been baptized, Jesus came up immediately from the water; and behold, the heavens were opened to him, and he saw the Spirit of God descending like a dove and alighting upon him. And suddenly a voice came from heaven saying, "This is my beloved son, in whom I am well pleased" (Mat. 3:16). In this scene we have:

- The Father, speaking from heaven, calling Jesus "My beloved Son."
- The Son, Jesus Christ, coming up from the water.
- The Holy Spirit like a dove descending from heaven and alighting upon the son.

The Koran also testifies to the existence of the Holy Spirit as a separate manifestation of the godhead. "We (Allah) gave Jesus the Son of Mary evidence, clear [signs] and strengthened him with the Holy Spirit (Koran 2:87). And: "To Jesus the Son of Mary We gave clear [signs], and strengthened him with the Holy Spirit (Koran 2:253). Ibn Katheir, the noted historian, cited Muslim theologian Ibn Abbas who said: "The Holy Spirit is the Greatest Name with which Jesus was able to raise the dead." He cited also Al Zamakhshari saying, "The Holy Spirit here means the Spirit of Jesus Himself" (Ibn Katheer, Volume 1, pages 117, 118). The Koran further declares that God is either visible or invisible and seats Him on a throne: "He (Allah) is the first and the last, and the outward (the visible) and the inward (the invisible); and he is the knower of all things. He is who created the heavens and the earth in six days; then he mounted on the throne" (Koran 57:3).

Why is it difficult for Muslims to believe that Jesus Christ is the Son of God when the Koran has incarnated and humanized God in many of its verses? This is tacitly clear in describing the Immaculate Conception: "And Mary, the daughter of Imran, who guarded her vagina (literal) and we breathed into it of our spirit . . ." (Koran 66:12). The idea of God having a son however is completely unacceptable in Islam for two main reasons:

1. The Bedouin mind cannot digest the idea of God fertilizing a human virgin to produce a human son directly related to Him. It even considers unacceptable to have a spirit—medium—fertilizing a human virgin. The Koran's account on the Holy Conception was and remains problematic to this day in the Muslim mind. On the one hand it states: "It would not be fitting to God that he should beget a son . . ." and on the other hand: ". . . When He determines a matter, He only says to it, "Be", and it is." (Koran 19:35); thus unquestionably assuring the recalcitrant mind of a God's 'fait accompli.'

2. The Ebionite belief and the "Gospel according to Hebrews" on which the Mecca Koran was based did not pronounce Jesus as the Son of God but a Prophet and "Head of the Angels". He was "not born but created by the God Father and is the first Archangel". The Koran's many narrations on Jesus revolve around this belief.

What pleases many Muslims is the Christian conviction that Jesus invariably addressed God as God as well as Father not only to himself but to all mankind. He clearly pointed to his disciples "I am going to my Father and your Father"; and when he called Himself the Son of God, so he called his disciples and listeners: "you are called the sons of God". And when he taught the Christians their daily prayer it was as is now: "Our Father who is in Heavens . . ." Furthermore, the unified Christian prayer or "Code of Belief" starts like this: "We believe in One God, Father, governing all, Creator of the heavens and earth, all seen and unseen . . ."

Therefore Muslims should accept that when Christians call themselves Sons of God they do not utter a blasphemy; they do so in the same manner and belief Jesus did and taught. This should in no way mean that Jesus or the rest of his followers are God's biological sons and therefore should not be branded as outright infidels. In as much as Jesus was constantly calling God His Father, and all Christians do that, He was also calling God his God and thus speaking of Him to his disciples. Most importantly, this is how he addressed Him while on the Cross in Aramaic: "Eli, Eli lima shabaktani . . ."—My God, My God why did you forsake me."

Why Muslims cannot accept these figurative and non physical approaches to God when the Koran itself abounds with them? The Koran gave God a face, a hand, an eye, and seated Him on the throne. Muslims may say this incarnation is allegorical and such expressions in the Koran are to be understood only in the sense that they are used in order to bring the infinite within the comprehension of the finite. They conclude that figurative incarnation is necessary for human beings to comprehend at least a glimpse of the Divine. This is exactly the Christian approach irrespective of its contingent dissimilarity. Here, the keen and unbiased Muslim mind can understand the basic confluence of both faiths that diverge in construal not in essence and manifestations not real meaning. Every time a Christian/Muslim parley convenes to discuss ways and means for a rapprochement, the above basic obstructions are avoided as taboo; generalities always deviate from the crucial subject and the outcome of every conference ends up inconclusive and insignificant.

NINETEEN

Enmities with the Jews

"Of the cities of these people, which the Lord your God does give you for an inheritance, you shall save alive nothing that breathes."

Bible

". . . And that day, every tree and stone will tell: here Muslim, behind me is a Jew for you to come and kill . . ."

Hadith & Koran

The war atrocities commended by God in old Palestine replicated by seemingly the same God later in Medina, Arabia and Palestine where they are now replayed, constitute an endless cycle of violence with historical magnitude. Attacks and counter attacks between Palestinians and Israelis have shown that this cannot be the way to peace. What it really shows is a history-repeating-itself of 400 biblical warring years between the same two peoples for the same cause. Today both sides are armed with verses more lethal than bullets from their respective religious arsenals. Both sides feel they have to take revenge because innocents on their sides had fallen.

The religious Zionists and Islamists both feel that the suffering of their people lies heavy upon them. Zionists remember not only the boisterous horrors of the Holocaust but the centuries of mistreatment before that. Islamists make no effort to understand the social causes of the suffering sustained by their people. Both parties regard themselves as having a special place in God's scheme of things. They are the "Chosen People of God" on one camp and the "Best Nation Brought out to People" on the other. God singled them both out for special instructions and a prescribed mission. It looks as if God picked this piece of land called Palestine, proclaimed his three monolithic religions as divide-and-rule time schemes and disappeared. Is He now up there watching with mixed emotions what His own hands have done?

Fundamentalists on both sides believe they have a mandate from heaven; both opposing mandates are self-destructive. Israel bristles with the most modern arms and possesses biological, chemical, and nuclear weapons; its presence still considered as an occupying power makes the entire region a powder keg and places in danger the lives of its peoples including the Jews who came to it as a haven. Displaced Palestinians in and outside suffer a tremendous dilemma of either a miserable life or an honorable death; the latter is frequently chosen. In each case the entire outside world is seen as an evil enemy to both, undifferentiated, unchanging, relentless "goyim" or "infidels", anti-Semitic or Islamphobic and this is the only explanation necessary.

Western governments explicitly believe the guilty needs to be punished. The displaced and angry believe with their supporters that the West is guilty and sacred jihad is due. While Western countries try to make sure they are punishing the guilty without sacrificing innocent lives in blind revenge, in most cases this turns out to be mission impossible. The loss of innocent blood is always staggering, causing more hatred and retribution through Jihad. The majority of Muslim populations are already destitute and suffering under their systems; punishing the guilty in blind revenge always carries dire consequences.

Jews and Muslims may be bracing for another 400 years of modern biblical warring if religion-fuelled antagonism remains uncontrolled. To Jewish religious fanatics the justification for the oppression of a people who had lived from time immemorial in a land that was promised them by God three millennia ago, is guided in their actions by the spirit if not by God's instructions in the Bible to ancient Israelites. Islamists insist Al-Qods, Jerusalem, is their third holy city, Muhammad's first prayer Kiblah (beacon) and his stop-over aboard Al-Buraq on his flight from Mecca to Heaven. His followers were the liberators of Palestine from the Romans.

The drama unfolds almost daily in the United States and Europe. While many courageous Israeli reservists refuse to serve in the occupied territories stating: "We will not go on fighting . . . for the purposes of domination, expulsion, starvation and humiliation of an entire people," religious zealots in Israel and the United States willfully blind themselves to the gross human rights violations of the occupation forces. In addressing a pro-Israel rally, Paul Wolfowitz, a leading Jewish hawk in the Bush administration thought it politically advisable to devote a sentence in his speech to the suffering of the Palestinians; he was roundly booed.

The smug arrogance that comes from the overwhelming American power provide further fuelling to Islamic fundamentalists, expressed in suicidal desperation born of poverty and oppression. It drives them to strike out at an enemy immensely more powerful than they are, in actions that they regard as one-way tickets to paradise. In Israel and elsewhere these actions have taken the form of suicide bombings, inhumane in its killing of innocent civilians including children. But Israeli state terrorism has killed far more children and other civilians in suppressing resistance with what Amnesty International has called "excessive and disproportionate use of force." This is an endless Machiavellian drama where all justifications are readily available.

Because of the violent conflict between Muhammad and the Jews in the seventh century extreme anti-Jewish motifs were already found in the Koran and within the Hadith tradition. Even though expressions refer to Jews as 'pigs, monkeys, servants of the devil and liars,' one should not draw hasty conclusions. For long periods the Jews fared better in the Islamic world than in Christian countries. After the 'second exodus' from Spain, Muslim Morocco was the Jewish safe haven. There were undoubtedly ups and downs yet never in the Middle Ages did the Jews under Islamic rule suffer as they did in Christian Europe.

Arab anti-Semitism has been the natural product of the Palestinian conflict. If a political solution for it could have been found some 30 years ago it could have been quelled. Today it has unfortunately become an integral part of the intellectual and cultural discourse of the Arab world. Much of Arab societies believe it and it is now much harder to uproot than in earlier stages.

Even for Egyptian intellectuals today many years after the Peace Treaty, Israel's existence represents an admission of the defeat in the Arab national vision. It is a confession that Egypt has failed to realize its historical destiny and greatness. The anti-Semitism slogan is acceptable among Arabs only if it comes from non Arabs as they themselves are Semites as well. While it is a disaster to the Jews it is a sickness to the Arabs; it prevents them from confronting their historical reality and absolves them from dealing with their own major failures. They are thus likely to remain in their pitiable situation.

All Palestinians and most Arab countries neighboring Israel believe that Zionism is poised to take over the rest of Jerusalem, its holy sites and continue thereafter step by step to achieve its entire control over Palestine. Most of them believe Israel at a later stage will invade Jordan, Syria, Lebanon and the rest of the Arab states. This is the likely future scenario unless Arabs take serious steps to confine Israel within prescribed and final borders. If the Arabs ignore the danger threatening them with destruction and avoid taking the necessary action they will share the same fate as that of their Palestinian brothers. This standpoint is opposed by a similar Israeli scenario: should Israel grant the Palestinians their state of Gaza, the West Bank and East Jerusalem the next Palestinian aim would be to reclaim again the whole of Palestine and cast the Jews back to Europe.

Here lies the controversial aspect of the conflict. Even if America is successful in throwing a credible "road map" accord it would be a fragile and deficient scheme. On the one hand historical and modern enmities among the two peoples cannot be wiped away in a meeting or convention; secondly the Palestinian 'diaspora' is on the lookout to return to its old homes, many of them still hold the keys of their old houses. Failure to achieve that will have one and only resort: Jihad—or terrorism in its modern name.

TWENTY

Islam, the Alien

"Islam started alien and will return as alien as it started, blessed are the aliens."

Muhammad

Whenever I am confounded with the arduous dilemma of the contemporary Muslim mind I immediately recall this mysterious lament by the Prophet later in his life. This is one prophecy of Muhammad I wish will never be fulfilled; first it is impossible to erase 1400 years of cherished tradition and secondly, aliens have no place in this globalization outburst today; they are simply unwelcome intruders.

These words saturated with regret, bitterness and guilt were frequently repeated and accompanied by another distressing saying: "Islam shifted from a faith into a Caliphate then on to a sinister Empire." What did Muhammad really regret and why he was so bitter about the metamorphosis of a mission that he started and propagated in a straight, unsoiled and peaceful endeavor.

Did this guilt emanate from the fact that he betrayed Waraka the 'Skillful Erudite', his spiritual guide and tutor? Was the regret ensued by following Abu Bakr's scheme for armed jihad carefully crafted and supported by the other tycoons in the Consultative House? Or was he bitter with the unchallenged dictates of arrogant Omar that he had to ingest even on his deathbed?

Was he sorry to have yielded to the Founding Fathers, helplessly watching them develop their grand schemes of an Arab domination powerhouse? The ailing and waning Prophet must have suffered deeply but stoically such alienation. He was sorry to see his nephew Ali playing a marginal, small fry role through the ongoing power struggle. A role he could not boost without highly disputed bias.

Or was he disappointed to see among his retinue false Muslims like Muawia, son of his staunchest enemy Abu Safian, who never really believed his Message and advised his descendents not to but only pretend so in order to reap the political domination? Did he realize that the Sufi Ebionite belief he acquired in 20 long years of learning and contemplation that he tried to promulgate in Mecca was contradicted and doomed in Medina where militant Islamic governance took over, delivering a conflicting and volatile scripture with various facets and interpretations?

Most historians agree and keep repeating that Muhammad was deeply gratified of an accomplished mission: he was speaking and behaving at all times with the ease of a man who has long since fought his most meaningful battles. But apparently that was skimming on the surface. Deep down Muhammad endured his dreadful alienation that bugged his childhood and accompanied him—and his mission—to the end of his life.

In fact Muhammad suffered alienation all over and with each and every person he was in touch with: he had nothing in common with his aged uncle and raiser Abu Taleb; he was the obedient student of sophisticated and haughty Waraka that he could distance himself from only after the Bishop's death; he was alienated sexually and emotionally from Khadija who could only give him financial and maternal protection and a high-up mansion that he never felt was home; he had his distance from his best friend Abu Bakr when he saw him betraying Waraka and charting his Consultative House plans. He felt his bitter alienation when he left his beloved Mecca to Medina and was further affixed to atrocious Omar who assumed his bulldozer approaches toward people and situations.

The Prophet's alienation widened with wives he struggled to control and a Medina politicking and warring Islam he tried hard to manage, to the extent of indoctrinating many "inspired" revelations to satisfy the whims of his entourage. His intensive sex indulgence did not dissipate his isolation but rather increased it while consuming his human machine. Clearly Muhammad became an outsider to what was going on through the prescribed tunnel of his warring moguls and companions. Hence his sorrowful repetition: "Islam shifted from a faith into a Caliphate then to a sinister Empire."

Muslims have undoubtedly inherited through ages a great deal of this estrangement. Their thinkers, identifiable by their various pulpits, carry the major role to defend, brace and quarantine their faith safely from the Western viruses of freedom, looseness and inventiveness. This inherited seclusion has become running in the blood. The more the world at large builds bridges of networking the more obstacles no matter how shabby, the Muslim mind creates.

The tragic irony is that classical Islam did recognize the existence of domains distinct from theology. Islam was meant and is still considered befitting both "faith and life" at the same time. That very recognition enabled several generations of Muslim scholars to dig into the Greek, Persian and Indian philosophical and cultural heritage in order to enrich the Islamic thought out of its seclusion. An ancient globalization of sorts that somehow brought out Islam from alienated trenches to an open world collaboration. That digging however touched only the peripheries of the faith without penetrating the core.

Many theopolitical discourses were designed to limit freedom of thought and expression in the Muslim world. An old, renewed phenomenon developed by militant thinkers set to oppose the Western influence and domination. It was unfortunately a negative, reactionary thinking and a neo-radicalism that revived Islam's extremism to propagate intolerance and confrontation; a further step back to alienation. Many moderate Muslims denounce Islamic terrorism and strive for a more tolerant and open interpretation of Islam. Many among those however learned their moderation from contact with the West. Their tolerance is barrowed and artificial because their current Islamic culture does not produce by itself such broad-mindedness. In most Muslim countries citizens are not exposed to the teachings of other religions. In fact they are encouraged to despise others' beliefs although ignorant of their true substance. Anyone who challenges such policy and take to comprehend another faith may suffer grave consequences. With this overwhelming attitude the moderate Muslim voice will always be curtailed and Islam will continue to be a vehicle for uninformed hatred of the non-believers.

In that sense the challenge most Muslims face today is a political rather than a religious one. It is perfectly possible for Muslims to develop a modern and democratic society in the era of globalization only if they shift from theopolitics to independent governance the way Turkey is now doing. To do that they have to accept that religion is a smaller part of life not the other way round as the religious discourses suggest. Sadly though, any leading debate in that direction would miss its purpose and collapse under the wrath of the demagogues.

Yet it is worth getting started. The Middle East as a natural inheritor of Islam sleeps and rises on repetitive prayers. Its peoples ruminate their prestigious past awakening from their tombs Abu Bakr, Omar, Othman, Ali and their descendents, asking their intercession while they, like insolvent merchants, revise their old and dilapidated books. This ongoing performance plunked the Islamic nations in a permanent autopsy room for foreign hands to dissect and dislocate. Their salute is no more in their hands and it became clear that in any debate Muslims rush to regard their world as a victim of injustice, misunderstanding and unfair propaganda. Many would lash out against "Islamphobia," noticeably growing in the West with tacit encouragement from powerful "lobbies."

As to the question of what role Islam has in the era of globalization the readily vague and defensive answer would arise: the Muslim world ridden with internecine feuds and conflicts with the West is in deep crisis. Any time it is necessary to take a clear position on terrorism and suicide bombing thinkers would weasel out and become demagogic pirouettes. Why the Muslim mind is unable to confront the truth and focus on concrete issues? Why any conference to discuss basic issues drifts into the uncertain seas of obfuscation? Conspiracy theories are the waves where dead souls assume the captaincy of phantom vessels.

Once Muslims set aside such theopolitical parley they could rid themselves of this shrouding alienation and acknowledge the distinction between Islam as a faith and Islam as an existential reality. This would enable them to shield Islam against rational and systematic criticism aimed at discovering its weaknesses and suggesting ways to correct them. In that way any critique of their lifestyles can no longer be condemned as a critique of Islam as a religious dividing line.

The many hurdles opposing this constructive thinking are there and obvious: liberty, social justice, equality, democracy, secularism, independence, mutual respect, free exchange and human rights are only existent by names. Suppression, injustice, inequality, subjugation, theo-dictatorship, flogging and stoning are the familiar sights among the true Muslim countries. Omar once spoke to people in Medina: "Do not ever undermine the stoning verse or say we could not find dual punishment (lashing and stoning) in the Koran. The Prophet had stoned and so do we." Many modern Muslims are not nostalgic to this practice; they do believe it belongs to an era long gone. But many others are; they hate to see any deviation from the original faith.

The Ulema have been staunch in reviving and implementing the past while in fact these same Ulema have been as much the victims of despotism in Muslim countries as any other social stratum. A case could be argued that the tragedies the Muslim world has suffered in the past 150 years were a result not of any action by the Ulema but of despotism in which the military, the self-styled peddlers of Western ideologies and sections of the urban middle classes were in the driving seat.

Once the blame game is set aside one should acknowledge the existence of politics, economics and ethics as domains distinct from theology. What this means is that political, economic and ethical issues cannot be defined, analyzed, understood and answered in purely theological terms. This is the single most important concern Islam lacks today. The denial of those distinct domains has enabled despots and demagogues of various ideological shades to invent a theopolitical discourse that prevents any rational discussion of the problems Muslims face today.

Islam will confront for many years to come a Western world superior in science and technology, stronger economically but largely secular in outlook and unattractive to many Muslims as a model of society. While modern Muslim thinkers welcome scientific progress and the Western values of equality and the rule of law, orthodox scholars stress the need to incorporate these within a strong, ethical framework based on the Koran and the words and deeds of Muhammad. Thus the continuous debate and struggle between "Westernized" and traditionalists will prove harmful. The avenues for imminent solutions to put this alienation at bay look indefinite.

Initiatives trickling from the Christian side are seemingly ineffective: The Second Vatican Council agreed that God and Allah were identical and made overtures. Discussions on ecumenism continue in Europe and the U.S yet progress is limited. To a Muslim, his own faith is the ultimate revelation of God to mankind. If he is devout he should have no doubt that Jews and Christians were offered the "true faith" and misunderstood it; they are too unaware of Islam's achievements in the past, its contributions to mathematics, science and medicine a thousand years ago and its domination of much of the old world until the last 300 years. The West remembers mainly the medieval crusades against Islam, the decadence of the Ottoman Empire and the Turkish indulgence in genocide against Christian Armenians at the turn of last century. It sees deviant Iran as constant threats to Israel as well as to one-sixth of the world's oil supplies.

Western critics of Muslims also argue that many of them are out of touch with the modern age and remain deep in transition. Traditional values clash with modern economics and third-world poverty, hunger and overcrowding. Islamic governance is generally successful when maintained by a one-man rule. Truly, Muslims need to redefine their identities in the face of modern technology and science. Islam has a serious personality crisis: its prerogative now is to accept the West as the Chinese and Japanese had done or offer its religious approach which is not in demand any more in this globalized market. However should conservative Islam absorb and assimilate modernism, the result would be a civilization with power restrained by ethical values and moral standards.

Any serious debate on how Islam relinquishes alienation and joins tomorrow's requirements must start with an end to the demagogic blame game. Perhaps the real battleground for Islamic openness is in the school itself. The kind of academic orientation students receive today determines their future inclinations. Some speakers retort the blame on the usual suspects of modern Islamic mythology: the Crusaders, the Orientalists, the Imperialists, the Zionists, the liberals, the secularists and so on. They did not realize that by identifying any of those usual suspects as author of the Islamic predicament they were absolving generations of Muslim intellectual and political leaders of their share of responsibility. They were not prepared even to discuss the tragic failure of such supposedly "Islamic" systems as in Iran, the Sudan and Afghanistan Taliban in the past three decades. Would they be prepared one day to blame the Islamist regimes in Libya, Tunisia and Egypt for their looming failures? The answer is readily available: no!

The major export of such Muslim countries today are hordes of angry, hungry, destitute and oppressed refugees whisked to the West under darkness or across raging seas seeking food and freedom. They search for and find political and human asylum where human rights are respected. The merciful West grants them refuge with little knowledge of the injected bane they always carry: 'play the meek until you have the upper hand"—slowly but surely the hungry wolves would rise to assert their place in their new societies and enforce their Jahilyia-inherited assessments, exploiting Western democratic tolerance to impose their quantitative power. Slowly but surely Western countries are getting their time bombs and Muslims their added dose of alienation. The now sleeping meek would emerge sooner or later to display their inner identity surely not in knowledge, science or construction and another 'Andalusia' tragedy would unfold with calamitous outcomes to their original countries and the rest of the Islamic world.

Perhaps time is now imminent for Islamic thinkers to avert such disaster. It lies in reformulating an Islam devoid of the prevailing bombarding textual hatred. Othman used these verses to restrain defeated civilizations; they had served their old purposes for better or worse. Some of their negative consequences still echo their encumbrance on Muslims today. Those Muslims should rise to dredge out all of the old controversies that alienated them throughout history, maintain all the tolerance and compassion of the Koran and chart their course in the modern human itinerary.

TWENTY ONE

Sufism in Islam

"He who has known his self has known Allah."
Muhammad

"O you soul which are at peace, return unto your Lord, pleased and satisfied. Enter among My worshippers and enter My Paradise."
Koran

T hus the Mecca Koran defined the state of the human soul ready to enter paradise: *"a soul at peace,"* the essence of Ebionite and Christian teaching to bestow orderliness upon the human life and establish an "outward" harmony. Man could then return inwardly to his Origin by means of the journey toward the "interior" way. This function is especially true in the original Islam; it has that divine injunction to establish order within the human soul and boost the interior life to prepare the soul to return unto its Lord and enter the Paradise which is a mixture of sensual pleasure and divine beatitude.

Islam transmuted from a 'faith', loving and glorifying the one and only God, into a 'Caliphate' conquering the far reaches of the known world and later into a 'sinister Empire' that like all man-made empires flourished, endured and withered down. As early as few years after its first inception, there was a nostalgic return to the moral fiber of the Mecca Koran and the Ebionite spirit of the Hira Cave. The movement was not known as the Sufism we know today.

The name comes from *Suf* (صوف), the Arabic word for "wool" in the sense of "cloak", referring to the simple cloaks the original Ebionite Sufis wore. *Tasawafa* is the Arabic verb deriving from *Suf,* and Sufi expresses the hidden meanings, simultaneously taken for 'occlusion' and 'enlightenment' to let the spirit soar up towards divinity itself. This journey is referred to as the path (*tariqa*). While all Muslims believe they are on the pathway to God and will become *close to Him in Paradise* after death and the "Final Judgment," Sufis are one step ahead: they believe it is possible as well to become close to God and truly experience this closeness . . . while alive on this earth.

The Sufi mystique must follow a path of deprivation and meditation; again an Ebionite far cry. There are various forms of abstinence and poverty. Worldly things are renounced and a complete trust in God's will is taught. The goal is to attain a higher knowledge and experience of Allah. The mystical focus meant that the Koran could be interpreted in different ways to bring to light the mystical meanings hidden within its pages. Out of this mysticism a type of pantheism developed among some Sufi believers. Pantheism is the teaching that God and the universe are one. Of course the orthodox Sunni Muslims who embrace the worldly aspects of Islam reject this idea since they maintain that Allah is the creator of the universe though conspicuously distinct from it. Sufism arose in part as a reaction to the growing Islamic materialism that had engulfed the Empire at that time. Islam had achieved great power and geographical scope promulgated by the Medina Founding Fathers and with it the material gain was enormous and streaming.

This mystical tradition where followers seek inner spiritual knowledge of God developed around the 10th century and has since fragmented into different orders: Ahmadiyya, Qadariyya, Tijaniyya, etc. The Sufis believe their roots can be traced back to the inception of Islam in the early 6th century as a result of the intense contemplation practiced by the Prophet in Waraka's Hira cave and have since followed a path of seclusion and meditation.

For Sufis, God is at once the First (*al-awwal*) and the Last (*al-akhir*), the Outward (*al-zahir*) and the Inward (*al-batin*). By function of His outwardness He creates a world of separation and otherness and through His inwardness He brings humans back to their Origin. Religious spirituality is the means whereby this journey is made possible from God and returns unto Him. Spiritual Islam as well as Christianity consists of another dimension besides *Tariqah* (the Path), ushered in by *Haqiqah* (the Truth). From another point of view they both correspond to *Islam*, *iman*, and *ihsan*, or "surrender", "faith" and "virtue".

Among all ethnic diversities who embraced Islam, only Arab Sufis developed a special momentum noticeable in a continuous attraction in their hearts exerted by God, pulling them in love towards Him. They experienced the joyful ecstasy of being gently drawn to their Eternal Beloved and saw themselves to be on a journey toward Heavens. In order to guide spiritual travelers and express the states of consciousness experienced throughout, they produced an enormously rich body of literature and often used a specialized technical vocabulary; they follow the path toward God primarily by means of love. They are enraptured with the love of a Creator, overall Master of all existence and Beautiful extraordinaire. Anyone not in love with God to this degree will not see what is so awesome about existence.

Within Islam Sufism has a distinguished position as well as a controversial one. It is at once a popular yet an occult form of Islam. Although followers are called *mu'mins*, from *iman* (faith) not all those who are *mu'mins* possess *ihsan*, the virtue and beauty enabling man to penetrate into the inner meaning of religion. The initial Islamic revelation is meant for all human beings destined to follow this tradition. But not all men are meant to follow the interior path. By following the Divine Will and die in grace man enters into Paradise. But there are those who yearn for the Divine while on earth and whose love for God and propensity for the contemplation of the Divine

Realities compel them to seek the path of inwardness. They do so by upgrading their *iman* into *ihsan* and "return unto their Lord with gladness" while still walking among men.

Mecca embraced the true spirituality of the faith: "Say (unto them): I exhort you unto one thing only: That you awake, for Allah's sake, and then reflect." And: "Lo! In the creation of the heavens and the earth and the difference of night and day are tokens (of His sovereignty) for men of understanding." (Koran). In Mecca, the Prophet disseminated such spirituality when he said: "The earth will never lack forty men similar to the Friend of the Merciful (Abraham), and through them people receive rain and are given help. None of them dies except Allah substitutes another in his place." (Narrated by Anas—Prophet Companion).

In Medina Muhammad moved from the Hira contemplation philosophy into the daily statehood humdrums, political feuds and armed Jihad engagements. He encouraged down-to-earth intellectual reasoning and singled out Sufi practice; declaring: "True worship does not lie in engaging oneself constantly in supererogatory prayers or in fasting copiously, but in contemplation of the creation and seeking to know the Creator through His works." By contradicting the early spiritual aspects he knocked down his early Ebionite piousness. Many poets copied the Prophet's remarks to ridicule the Sufi practitioners. Example:

> "He went on imploring the Almighty in the night
> All alone under cover of darkness . . . and fright,
> A poor hermit, whose hermitage, in pious recoil,
> Consumed to the bones both his body and soul.

Crying O utmost Hope, save me from falling
Because of my repeated sins and tragic failing
I am but a slave, afflicted by false hope
And now see death strangling me with its rope . . ."

Ali on the other side, who grew up with the initial spiritual faith, retained his devout communion with the soul. Amongst the close companions of the Prophet there were those, like Abu Dharr Ghaffari, Miqdad, the Ebionite Salman the Persian and a few others who became staunch followers of Ali and spread his teachings of gnosis. If Ali had been allowed to succeed the Prophet it is very likely that gnosis would have grown as an integral part of Islamic faith without any mantle of additional rituals. The Consultative House leaders however were bent on outstretching and managing the Empire when Ali failed to assume the Caliphate; the governing Omayad regimes that followed were often unfavorable and at time violently hostile to those who practiced or preached spirituality. They divested Islam of its original sanctity and used it as a power machine to attain their political goals. Under those circumstances gnosis assumed a distinct and separate form under a thick concealment mantle.

The growth and development of piety and spirituality amongst early Muslims was in fact the result of the tyranny of those rulers who seized the helm of the Empire before and after the death of Ali in 40 Hijrah. The old Meccan *Ayah* was ever alive in their minds: "Such as remember Allah, standing, sitting, and reclining, and consider the creation of the heavens and the earth, (and instinctively cry out): Our Lord! You created not this in vain! Glory be to You! Preserve us from the doom of Fire." (Koran 3.190). This they were able to do with a fragile impunity especially that following the death of the Prophet, Ali had been denied succession. On the other hand it is also believed that had the people accepted Ali as the rightful successor, there would not have been such extensive rise of spirituality as Ali would probably have followed the Consultative House preoccupation path towards the 'Sinister Empire.'

In addition to its law and the esoteric aspect contained in Sufism and gnosis, Shia inherited and pursued the Divine Wisdom from the Prophet and the Imams which became the basis for the *hikmah* that later developed extensively in the Muslim world and incorporated elements of Greco-Alexandrian, Indian and Persian intellectual heritages. In this context the Muslim mind owes this movement its major openness on reasoning and assimilation. The Shia Imams and their close followers led a highly spiritual life and expressed sacred ideas in the context of Islam through supplications, lectures and other writings. They were not known as Sufis as the term later came to be understood. Their saintly life abounded with piety and, having traversed through comprehension the formal and philosophical aspects of the faith, they sought to unveil the Truth through intellectual reasoning. They neither renounced the world nor assumed any formal identity. Their teachings often attracted adherents from the Sunni schools of thought with the result that it is common today to find Sunni Sufi groups aligned with the school of the Shia spiritual masters. Notable among such groups is the Naqshbandi order.

While *Shariah* governs all of man's outward life as well as his body and psyche, the Sufi path leads beyond the usual understanding of the "soul" as a separated and forgetful substance. In Sunni Islam this dimension is almost completely identified separately from general practices; while in Shia Sufism aspects are intermingled within the general structure of the religious doctrines and practices themselves. There exists an intermediate region between the obvious and the mysterious: a world of practice and doctrines that are reflections of the inner teachings of Sufism and a foretaste of its riches.

Many of the Sunni prayer manuals which occupy a high position such as the *Dalail al-khayrat* (the Signs of Bounties), were written by Sufi masters; while in the Shia world almost all the prayers such as the *al-Sahifah al-sajjadiyyah* (the Prostration Funnel) of the fourth Imam Zayn al-Abidin, partake of both an obvious and a mysterious character. Occasionally there has even been the penetration of one domain upon another such as the sayings of many of the Imams, which have appeared in Sufi writings that penetrated Shiite prayers identified with some of the Imams like Abdullah Ansari of Hera, Iraq, who crossed the threshold of sanctity. His *Munajat* (Supplications) are deep yearnings of the heart for the Infinite and devotion prayers chanted with the deepest of emotions.

A typical Sufi supplication goes like this: "Guide us on the straight path, (Koran). Namely eliminate from us the darkness of our states so that we can become illuminated by the lights of Your sanctity and leave behind having been overshadowed by the phantoms of our seeking. And raise from us the shadow of our striving, so that we can gain vision by the stars of Your generosity and find You through You."

Sufis assert that the attainment of the knowledge that comes with such intimacy with Allah is the very purpose of the creation. Here they mention the *hadith qudsi* in which God states, "I was a hidden treasure and I loved that I be known, so I created the creation in order to be known." Hence for the Sufis there is already a momentum, a continuous attraction on their hearts exerted by God pulling them in love towards Him. They experience the joyful ecstasy of being gently drawn to their Eternal Beloved.

Sufis do not see any offence in involving the Beloved God in their earthly matters. In fact they communicate with Him in both prose and poetry as they do with a trusted friend:

> **You created female beauty for us and said:**
> **My worshippers refrain, do not be led . . .**
> **You are Beautiful and a true beauty lover**
> **How could passion cease in Your follower!**

Two most famous Sufi specimens may be introduced with details, **Rabi'a al-Adawyia** among women and **Hasan al-Basri** among men. They had intermingling lives; they exemplify and clarify the many aspects of Sufism.

Rabi'a al-Adawiya is certainly the most famous woman poet and Sufi. Her father Ismail married her mother and went to live on the edge of the desert not far from the town of Basra, Iraq. They had four daughters in a raw, the fourth was Rabi'a.

Ismail died when she was 11 leaving behind his wife and four daughters all of whom were very poor. The mother now alone, decided to take her four daughters out for Basra where she hoped to make a better living. On their way they were set upon by bandits and in defense of her family the mother was killed and each of the daughters was taken as a slave by the robbers; Rabi'a was sold in Baghdad.

She was very beautiful with a lovely voice so her master taught her how to sing, play the 'oud', dance and entertain people making good money for him. Through this career she developed many bad habits, living a very low life amongst all sorts of people and not caring about anything that she did. This continued until she was about thirty-six years old when one day as she was singing at a wedding she found herself singing in a different way. Unworldly songs were coming from her heart expressing divine Love. Allah had awakened Rabi'a.

From that moment she refused to sing, dance or play any music for anyone except for her Beloved God. Her master was very angry because he could no longer exploit her. He began to ill-treat and beat her into returning to her former ways. But she refused. Seeing that he could not influence her in any way he decided to resell her. So he put a cord around her neck and took her to the slave market of Baghdad. A good man there took Rabi'a to his home, gave her food and simple clothes and told her that he did not want anything from her except that she could pray and be free in his house. Rabi'a thanked him with all her heart and said "If you want anything from me for the Face of Allah, He will give you your reward; but if you want anything from me for yourself only I have nothing to give you."

Enter **Hasan al-Basri.**

Hasan was born in Medina in the year 642 B.C. to a servant of the Prophet's wife Om Sulma and a freedman of Zaid bin Thabit, Muhammad's stepson. As a young child he had lived with his mother in Om Sulma's household. In manhood he followed a follower of Ali who never ceased to propagate his original Ebionite theories. Hasan is usually referred to as being one of the closest of the Sufis around Rabi'a in her life. He is recorded as the person who proposed to marry her, to which she replied: "The tie of marriage is for those who have being. But here being has disappeared for I have become as nothing to myself and I exist only through Allah for I belong wholly to Him and I live in the shadow of His control. You must ask for my hand from Him and not from me."

Hasan replied, "How did you find this secret, Rabi'a?"

She answered, "I lost all found things in Him."

Hasan asked, "How did you come to know Him?"

She said, "You know of the how but I know of the howless."

Like many of the ascetic Sufis, Rabi'a made no separation in her love between man and woman if they lived for the Face of God. She had many followers who yearned to feed themselves from her Love which she gave to all those whom she loved. It is said Rabi'a used to kneel a hundred times daily saying, 'I ask for no recompense but only to satisfy the Almighty God.' One of her poems:

Your hope in my heart is the rarest treasure
Your Name on my tongue is the sweetest pleasure
My choicest hours of the night and day
Are those hours I spend with You . . . and stay.

O God, can I survive this world of turmoil
without remembering You, to ease my daily toil
How can I endure the next world, the hereafter
without seeing Your face and gladden ever after

I am estranged here, stranger in Your earth
lonely among worshippers, alien to their dearth
Hence my supplication, give me faith and hope
Support my complaint and let my ordeal stop!

Rabi'a also wrote many heart-stirring fables. A specimen:

"I saw myself in a wide green garden more beautiful than I could begin to understand. In this garden was a young girl. I said to her: "How wonderful this place is!"

"Would you like to see a place even more wonderful than this?" she asked. "Oh yes," I answered. Then taking me by the hand she led me on until we came to a magnificent palace like nothing that was ever seen by human eyes. The young girl knocked on the door and someone opened it. Immediately both of us were flooded with light.

God alone knows the inner meaning of the maidens we saw living there. Each one carried in her hand a serving tray filled with light. The young girl asked the maidens where they were going and they answered her: "We are looking for someone who was drowned in the sea and so became a martyr. She never slept at night, not one wink! We are going to rub funeral spices on her body."

"Then rub some on my friend here," the young girl said.

'Once upon a time," said the maidens, "part of this spice and fragrance clung to her body but then she shied away."

Quickly the young girl let go of my hand, turned and said to me:

"Your prayers are the lights that take you a full length;
Your devotion is the force that supports your strength;
Sleep and neglect towards both are the enmity.
And life can only give life: the sole opportunity.
If you ignore it or waste it you are certainly sure . . .
You will soon turn to dust and not live anymore . . ."

Then the young girl disappeared."

Rabi'a never married or had any children. She left Baghdad and returned to Basra where she remained for many years until she finally traveled to Jerusalem with an attendant woman and she bought a small house on top of the Mount of Olives. She used to walk down every day to al-Aqsa Mosque to give teachings to the people, both men and women, who would listen to her. This she did every day until she died in the year 801 B.C. Her followers built a tomb for her which still exists near the Christian Church of the Ascension on top of the Mount of Olives.

Despite her controversial and tumultuous early life she is often referred to as the first true female Saint (waliya) of Islam; whether her turning from worldly to Sufi living was stirred by repentance or inspiration. Rabi'a embodies the true Sufism with its absolute spiritual love. She inspired during and after her life many poets and writers. Khalil Gibran the famous philosopher/painter (The Prophet) is said to have been deeply enthused by Rabi'a's mysticism, he unleashed in his paintings the voices of the soul expressed by the naked body. In this same perspective she recites:

> "I have made You the Companion of my heart and soul.
> But my body is available to those who desire its company,
> My body is friendly to its guests, numerous and many . . .
> But the Beloved of my heart is the guest of my soul."

Many of the negative incidents recorded about Rabi'a's early life and her relationship with Hasan al-Basri have been termed irrelevant. Only her deeds and sayings are. She once sent Hasan a piece of wax, a needle and a hair and said: "Be like wax and illumine the world and burn yourself. Be like a needle and perform like a naked truth. When you have done these two things a thousand years will be for you like a hair."

She developed her own rite of Sufi doctrines. She once said: there are three kinds of men: The first believes that his hands and his sons' hands are all that is necessary to succeed in the only world they know—the material world. The second kind prays with his hands so that a reward will be earned in the next life. The third kind has his hands tied at the wrist, bound with love to serve without thought of return."

In this same approach she said:

> "O God, whatsoever You have apportioned to me,
> Of worldly things, give that to Your enemy,
> And what You have apportioned to me in the hereafter,
> Give that to Your Friends, You suffice me far better."

Her life and sayings became a source of deep inspiration for all those who were drawn to her and followed her both in her time and afterwards. Her single secret ingredient, love, manifesting directly without any trace of self in it, brought a special fragrance into the more austere teachings of those early Sufis. She was the Word which gave life to the hearts of those who followed after her in the same line.

Her poetic supplications are still masterpieces of heart-felt emotions put in words. She once wrote:

> "I love You with two loves—one, a selfish love
> And one worthy of You, above any other love.
> As for the selfish love, it is that I think of You,
> And exclude anything that looms besides You
> As to the Love that You are worthy of forever,
> Ah! That I see only You and no other creature ever,
> There is no praise for me in either aspects of love,
> The praise in both is for You who dwells above."

She also said:

> "God, if I worship You for fear of Hell burn me in Hell,
> And if in hope of Paradise exclude me from Paradise.
> But if I worship You for Your very own sake,
> Your everlasting Beauty will suffice me to take."

As to Hasan he was one of the great Hadith masters and narrators especially from Ali. He established in Basra the first school of self-disciplined asceticism. Hasan would comment on the Prophet's Hadith borrowed from Jesus: "The likeness of my Companions is like salt in food. Food is not good without it," and would compare himself and his followers to those disciples.

He was in continuous personal struggle against one's lusts—'jihad of the soul.' His doctrinal mainstay harbors two thoughts that roam over the soul, "one from Allah the other from Satan. Allah shows mercy on a servant who settles at the thought that comes from Him. Man embraces the thought that comes from Allah while he fights against the one from Satan. If man follows the dictates of anger and appetite the dominion of Satan appears in him through idle passions and his heart becomes the nesting-place and container to demons. If he does battle his passions to dominate his ego (*nafs*) imitating in this the character of the angels, at that time his heart becomes the resting place of angels and they alight upon it."

In this doctrine Hasan is inspired by the verses: "Nay, both His hands are spread wide, and He bestows as He wills" (Koran 5:64) and: "If you love Allah, follow me, and Allah will love you" (Koran 3:31), referring to Allah's kindness and goodness. He harshly categorizes worshippers: "the Reciters of the Koran are three types. The first type take the Koran as a merchandise by which to earn their bread; the second type uphold its letters and lose its laws aggrandizing themselves over their people and seeking gain through it from the rulers. Finally, the third type who sought the healing of the Koran of the sickness of their hearts, that kind is rarer than red sulphur!"

In this context Hasan did not hesitate to admonish the mighty Umayad Caliph Omar bin Abdul Aziz (717-720) and insinuate Sufism in a letter extolling asceticism:

"O Prince of Believers, beware of this world (*dunya*) with all wariness; for it is like a snake, smooth to the touch but its venom is deadly. The more it pleases you the more you be wary of it; for the man of this world whenever he feels secure in any pleasure thereof the world drives him over into some unpleasantness and whenever he attains any part of it and squats him down in it the world turns him upside down. And again beware of this world for its hopes are lies, its expectations false; its easefulness is all harshness.

"Muhammad he bound a stone upon his belly when he was hungry; and Moses was told: 'Moses, when you see poverty approaching say: welcome to the badge of the righteous!' And when you see wealth approaching say, Lo: a sin whose punishment has been looming.' If you should wish you might listen to the Lord of the Spirit and the Word [Jesus]. He used to say, 'My daily bread is hunger, my badge is fear, my raiment is wool, my mount is my foot, my lantern at night is the moon and my fire by day is the sun and my fruit and fragrant herbs are such things as the earth brings forth for the wild beasts and the cattle (the Ebionite lifestyle). All the night I have nothing, yet there is none richer than I!"

Like Rabi'a, Hassan had the gift of poetry:

In love, nothing exists between breast and breast.
Out of intense longing speech is born at its best.
True description differs from that real taste.
He, who tastes, attains fullness with no waste,
the one who explains lies in describing.
How to draw the true form of a specific something . . .

> in whose presence you are blotted out?
> And whose being you can't exist without?
> And who is a living sign for your transfer crossing?

As time passed many Sufi orders came into existence, each with its own *tariqah*, its own "guide" or "master" and its own expression form of spirituality. In this development they were influenced as we noted earlier not only by the Christian mystics but with their heritage of Ebionite spirituality established at the Hira cave by the "skillful erudite" and carried over not by Muhammad who found himself in Medina the de-facto leader of a growing kingdom; but by Ali who did not renounce to his early spiritual education with much of it inscribed in his book 'the Exemplar of Eloquence, and his companions and descendents who carried the Sufi torch after him.

Later as the Greek thinkers such as Plato, Aristotle and the Neo-Platonists introduced to the Arabs through Caliph Al-Mamun's famous academy 'Beit al Hikmah,' (the House of Wisdom), many orders that were influenced by the neo-Christian mystics renounced the world believing such renunciation to be a great act of piety and began to live in recluse as hermits. They were subjected to criticisms by the jurists from the Sunni schools in line with the Medina dictates. In some cases the Sunni regimes persecuted, imprisoned and even executed some leading Sufis. The chasm between the ruler-assigned theologians and the free lance Sufi masters began to widen and with certain theologians the Sufis today are on the other side of the spiritual divide beyond the rigors of Islam.

The Shia scholars and jurists on the other hand found a common ground in the Sufi spirituality based on practicing the beliefs along with the Sufi rituals which they did not perceive as anti-Islamic. To them the spirit of Imam Ali is still well and alive. One of their leaders, Fadlalla Haeri notes:

"The outer practices of the Sufis include varying amounts of prayers, invocations, recitations and supplications. We often find that not only the local ecology and physical environment had a lot to do with the type of Sufi practices which predominated in a certain area but also the culture, class and socio-economic conditions of the group which played the most prominent role in these practices. We find that some Sufi orders became almost exclusively for the well-off and the influential in the society. For example the Tijani Order in North Africa seems to have attracted those who were politically powerful while the Darqawi order has been predominantly followed by the poor." (The Elements of Sufism—page 44).

Islam today is in deep need of Sufi practitioners, brotherhoods and sisterhoods. They can be the effective antidotes to the widespread extremist movements and a recreation of the original Mecca Islam to harness the Medina dogmatic strays. Sufis beliefs and teachings are the essence of every religion and indeed of the evolution of humanity as a whole. These hidden and subdued hands of Islam can reach out and mend fences with the Christians in the East or West. They represent the human façade of a great faith initiated primarily on the bases of love and spirituality.

The central concept in Sufism is "love". It is a projection of the essence of God to the universe. God desires to recognize beauty and as if one looks at a mirror to see oneself, God "looks" at Himself within the dynamics of nature. Since everything is a reflection of God, Islam can display this reflection. The school of Sufism lives out to see the beauty inside the apparently ugly and to open arms even to most evildoers. This infinite tolerance is expressed in the most beautiful way perhaps, by the famous Sufi philosopher and poet Mevlana:

> "Come, come, whoever, wherever you are . . .
> Lover of Leaving, Worshiper, Wanderer;
> Ours is a caravan of hope, not despair.
> Though you broke your vows and undertaking,
> Come, come again, your new life is in the making."

While some Sufis like this poet become utterly consumed by the intensity of love, for most who wish to love God their love is merely a wavering flame ever in danger of diminishing. Hence, by remembering God's forgotten reality and beauty Sufis rekindle the flame of their love for God. In Sufism it is remembrance that makes the heart grow fonder. This is the perfect relationship between practice (*dhikr*) and love that constitutes the inner spirituality of Islam.

TWENTY TWO

Afterword

In this day and age the world is divided into two major camps: the bursting civilizations that are reaching out, expanding, bubbling with scientific ideas, economic plans, political and cultural expressions—and the other camps that are flinching, collapsing on themselves with economic, political and social crises that prevent any serious attempts for major initiatives. The former is overflowing with optimism and sights firmly fixed on the future; the latter is weighed down by their history, traditions, ethnic and religious revulsions.

Pious Muslims know that the problem with the globalizing civilization is the vacuum of moral philosophy where the heart should be. What gives the West its dynamic energy is individualism, the desire to dominate and the sheer drive to acquire material items through a philosophy of consumerism; such frenetic energy keeps societies moving.

Patience, slowness and equilibrium by contrast, are emphasized in Islam. "Haste is the devil's work", the Prophet warned. This age however is based on speed, intoxicated speed that presides over media, production and marketing of either tangible or intangible products. The unceasing noises, dazzling colors and shifting images are beckoning and harassing. Silence, withdrawal and old-style meditation are simply not today's merchandise.

The Muslim is restless at the modern universality of a media full of power and pervasiveness because of its malignity and hostility toward Islam. These intrusions corrode the innermost structure of the Oriental society based on family values. The crumbling authority structures of the West that have been under constant attacks are now contagious and easily communicable.

The apparent dilemma suffered by Muslims is to stop or go on dragging along the path of the West's social experimentation which they know it diverges from their own vision of society. They crave not to disrupt their domestic situation for temporary values; a difficult quest indeed and only Jihad can stand against such overpowering, immediate and glamorous appeals.

Yet Jihad with its scope to strive, to seek and not to yield, has become a dirty word in the media representing the physical threat of an incompatible civilization no matter how noble and powerful its concept may appear. This misunderstanding between Islam and the West nullifies the Muslim capability to respond coolly and meaningfully.

Hence the need to the introspection process by Muslims themselves. Islam is basically a religion of equilibrium and tolerance suggesting an encouraging breadth of vision and fulfillment of human destiny in the universe. The Muslim voices of learning and balance—in politics and among academics should not be drowned by those advocating violence and hatred. The crucial balance that should be thought out and maintained is between *din* (religion) and *dunya* (world); it is a balance of and not a separation between the two. Muslims have not been created for their religion and the exact opposite is true. They should live in the *now*, in the real world and not within the antiquated frame of postulations that pulls the mind from today's realities back to the nostalgic and tumultuous past.